Computer Capers

ALSO BY THOMAS WHITESIDE

Computer Capers

*Tales of Electronic
Thievery, Embezzlement,
and Fraud*

Thomas Whiteside

THOMAS Y. CROWELL COMPANY
Established 1834
NEW YORK

Most of the material in this book appeared originally in *The New Yorker,* in slightly different form.

COMPUTER CAPERS: TALES OF ELECTRONIC THIEVERY, EMBEZZLEMENT, AND FRAUD. Copyright © 1978 by Thomas Whiteside. All rights reserved. Printed in the United States of America. No part of this book may be used or reproduced in any manner whatsoever without written permission except in the case of brief quotations embodied in critical articles and reviews. For information address Thomas Y. Crowell Company, 10 East 53rd Street, New York, N.Y. 10022. Published simultaneously in Canada by Fitzhenry & Whiteside Limited, Toronto.

FIRST EDITION

Designed by Stephanie Krasnow

Library of Congress Cataloging in Publication Data

Whiteside, Thomas, 1918–
  Computer capers.

  Bibliography: p.
  1. Computer crimes. I. Title.
HV6773.W49   1978   364.1'62   77-25184
ISBN 0-690-01743-X

78 79 80 81 82 10 9 8 7 6 5 4 3 2 1

To Marie

Contents

Acknowledgment

Among the many computer scientists and computer-security specialists whom I have consulted in the course of the researches that have resulted in this book and for whose help I am grateful, I would like, in particular, to express my appreciation for the most generous cooperation extended to me by Donn B. Parker (author of *Crime by Computer*), of Stanford Research International, who kindly allowed me access to his extensive press-clipping files at S.R.I. bearing on particular computer-related crimes, and provided me with many valuable leads to other sources of information on this intriguing subject.

Thomas Whiteside

New York
January 1978

Computer Capers

1

The Attenuation of Money

Crime usually does its ingenious best to keep pace with technology, so it is probably inevitable that some of the more interesting specialized manifestations of criminality to emerge recently have had to do with deliberate misuses of the computer. Over the past two decades, computers have come to play such a dominant role in the processing of all kinds of information that it is now difficult to imagine any large-scale enterprise being able to function without them. In banking; in conducting credit transactions of every kind, including those involving credit cards; in keeping records of corporate sales; in drawing up inventories and payrolls; in trading securities; and in maintaining Social Security, health, welfare, and tax records—in all these activities the computer has become an essential organizational tool. Some 150,000 computers are currently in use in the United States, but that figure does not reflect the true extent of computerization in the country, for just one large computer may serve several thousand individuals or corporations, who, on a time-sharing basis, feed their particular programming data into it by telephone connection from remote keyboard terminals or other devices, and receive, via telephone line, printouts or other records of processed information. The number of Americans now directly involved in computer operations is more than two million. This group includes programmers, who translate written information into binary computer language and prepare it in step-by-step, logical form for electronic processing; operators who handle the computers themselves and their data-storage libraries; and operators at keyboard terminals and printout terminals.

The number of citizens whose lives are affected by computers is, of course, incomparably greater than this, for it includes practically everyone who has a bank account, engages in any kind of credit transactions, or has any kind of financial relationship with the government or with any large organization. In fact, one would have to be a hermit nowadays to avoid involvement in the economic and social consequences of computer-processing activity. To most people, the computer is a sort of unseen universal engine of unfathomable complexity—a device capable of calculating at incredible speed the correct path to land spacecraft on Mars, the status of one's bank account, or the seating available on a commercial-airline flight. It seems to possess an almost magical ability to produce certainty out of a box, and at the same time it endows what used to be transactions between human beings, which were slower and perhaps less efficiently conducted, with an air of chilling impersonality.

The intimidating effect of the computer is not confined to people who have only an ordinary citizen's knowledge of its functioning but often extends to managers and chief officers of big corporations that employ computers on a large scale. These executive types seem to be fascinated by the efficiency of computers and by the endless print-outs that can be ordered up at the touch of a button, and too often they tend to place in the veracity of these instant and apparently unassailable results a faith that they would almost certainly hesitate to place in the work of mere human beings. Even professional auditors seem frequently to give unusual credence to the accuracy of the computer printouts that form a large part of the evidence of an organization's financial position. Often an auditor's faith in the computer has led to surprises.

The impersonality of the computer also affects the people who are in the computer profession—who work as programmers or computer operators, or who staff remote terminals connected to the computers. But, having a working understanding of what computers can and cannot do, these people are less prone to intimidation by the computing process than are the managers of the corporations that employ them or the citizens the daily details of whose lives are now so largely subject to computer accounting and recording. It seems that a sort of computer mystique has helped make possible a significant increase in illegal manipulations of the computer, in which it and its technology have been used as instruments of embezzlement, fraud, and theft.

It also seems that computers have driven some people who work with them to crimes that have taken on the quality of ideological acts. A clear example, involving theft through a computer of what in this kind of crime is an altogether trifling sum—the equivalent of $720—was that of an English salary clerk named Henry King. In a court in Cambridge, he pleaded guilty to manipulating the computer programming for his company's salary accounts in such a way as to have the computer pay him salary checks to which he was not entitled. In his defense, his lawyer explained to the court that King had under- taken to outwit his company's computer because it was "a horrible impersonal machine."

Records of computer crime contain a number of instances in which the computer has been an object of physical attack, for the reason that someone has come to regard it either as a kind of electronic destroyer of personal identity or as an abhorrent symbol of corporate capitalism. Sometimes these attacks are committed by programmers or other computer processors in irrational outbursts, and sometimes they are planned, for political or other reasons. Several incidents have involved guns being fired at computers. In 1974, at an installation at the Charlotte Liberty Mutual Life Insurance Company, in Charlotte, North Carolina, a computer operator, apparently in a fit of frustration, was reported to have fired a handgun several times at the company computer. In Olympia, Washington, in 1968, an unknown person fired two shots from a pistol at an I.B.M. 1401 computer in a state employment office. And in a municipal office in Johannesburg, South Africa, in 1972, an unidentified person, who city officials suspected may have been the recipient of an exorbitant bill of some kind, fired four shots through a window at a computer. The computer was dented but continued working.

Where guns have not been used, attackers seem to have employed any instruments at hand to disable computers. After half a million dollars had been spent in attempts to correct fifty-six serious breakdowns over a two-year period in a Burroughs 3500 computer used by the National Farmers Union Service Corporation of Denver to process data from the Farmers Union insurance companies, a computer operator was arrested and accused of having caused the breakdowns by inserting a car key in a memory-disc file, thus short-circuiting the computer's memory. The suspect, who was caught in 1972 through the use of a closed-circuit television monitor, was subsequently quoted as telling police that he had committed the acts because of an "overpowering urge" to shut the computer down. A while later, in New York, a memory system in a Metropolitan Life Insurance Company computer was found to have been damaged by an attack with a screwdriver. And an attack in 1972 on the core memory system of a Honeywell computer used by a New York bank—this one evidently also carried out with a pointed instrument—caused damage to the computer estimated at $589,000.

Computers have also been the targets of sabotage by radical, revolutionary, or otherwise dissident groups. During the Vietnam war, a number of computer centers on American campuses—particularly those at universities reported to be engaged in Defense Department research—were bombed by radical students. On August 24, 1970, for example, a bomb exploded outside a building at the University of Wisconsin that housed the Army Mathematics Research Center and other research activities funded by the federal government. The explosion resulted in the death of one employee and injuries to three other people, and caused damage estimated at nearly $2.5 million. Computers at the research center were seriously damaged in the bombing, which also destroyed a twenty-year accumulation of computer data stored on the premises—this data alone representing an investment of about $16 million.

In the same year, a Molotov-cocktail bombing of a computer at Fresno State College, in California, caused damage estimated at $1 million. In 1973, antiwar demonstrators in Australia shot a computer in the offices of an American computer manufacturer in Melbourne. The weapon used was a double-barreled shotgun, and the damage to the computer was extensive. At New York University, in 1970, a group of radical students placed gasoline bombs on an Atomic Energy Commission computer being used by the university, and declared that they would destroy the computer unless they were given $100,000 to pay the bail bond of a jailed Black Panther. Faculty members raced into the computer room in time to defuse the devices.

During a six-month period in 1974, four attempts were made by unknown parties to sabotage computer operations at Wright-Patterson Air Force Base by means that included the use of magnets to destroy data stored on tape, the loosening of wires on the computer mainframe, and the gouging of electronic equipment with a sharp tool. However, the financial losses from these attempts were small.

An attack on an academic computer facility in Rome in June 1977 was more costly. According to a Reuters dispatch, three masked women, armed with rifles and a silencer-equipped pistol, held two professors and an assistant on duty powerless in a computer center at the university while a male accomplice poured gasoline on the center's computer and then set it on fire. The computer-terrorist women gave no motive for their behavior. Damage to the computer and the premises was estimated at more than $2 million.

This particular incident was only one of ten planned attacks on computer centers in Italy during 1976 and 1977. According to a Rome dispatch in *Computerworld* in August 1977, by E. Drake Lundell, Jr., most of these attacks appeared to have been organized by an armed terrorist group calling itself the Unita Combattenti Communiste. In five of the attacks where figures for the damage inflicted were available, the financial damage done averaged over $1 million per bombing. According to a raid-by-raid summary of this series of attacks presented in the *Computerworld* article, the first reported assault by the terrorist group occurred in May 1976, when a band of fifteen men, armed with handguns and submachine guns, invaded a local government tax office in Rome and threw ten Molotov cocktails among computer equipment installed there destroying eight I.B.M. 2740 terminals. This was followed by commando-style attacks during 1976 on computer installations at an Italian pharmaceutical company and the Milan offices of an Italian conglomerate, and, in 1977, on the computer installations in Rome of a steel manufacturing company, of a petrochemical company in Calabria, and on a computer center at the University of Bocconi. The attacks involved either burning the computers with gasoline or blowing them up with bombs, or both. In addition to all this, I.B.M.

and Honeywell Information Systems offices in Italy were also reported as having been subjected to terrorist attacks.

The impersonality of the computer and the fact that it symbolizes for so many a system of uncaring power tend not only to incite efforts to strike back at the machine but also to provide certain people with a set of convenient rationalizations for engaging in fraud or embezzlement. The computer lends an ideological cloak for the carrying out of criminal acts. Computer crime, to those who engage in it, is not like stealing a purse from an old lady; it imparts to theft a nice, clean quality. Except in actual physical assaults on computers, computer crime is seldom associated with overt violence. It also holds several other attractions for the potential lawbreaker. It provides intellectual challenge—a form of breaking and entering in which the burglar's tools are essentially an understanding of the logical structure of and logical flaws inherent in particular programming and processing systems. It opens the prospect of obtaining money by means that, while clearly illegal, do not usually involve taking it directly from the till or the cashier's drawer. In most large organizations, money that is kept on the premises is guarded far more strictly than the company computers and their contents are. In our computer-oriented society, however, the use of actual money has become less frequent; instead, its equivalent circulates vicariously, in the form of digital information on tapes or other storage devices. Only the proper application or manipulation of computer logic can convert these signals into real money, by directing them electronically to particular accounts, on which negotiable checks can be drawn. (More likely than not, the checks are made out by a computer.) The attenuation of money into digital impulses has probably contributed to the increasing incidence of waywardness among people who continually process so much of it in such a form.

Other tempting features of computer crime, as distinct from other forms of criminal activity, are that most such crimes are difficult to detect and that when the guilty parties *are* detected not much seems to happen to them. For various reasons, they are seldom intensively prosecuted, if they are prosecuted at all. On top of these advantages, the haul from computer crime tends to be very handsome compared with that from other crimes. For example, the average take in armed bank robberies committed in this country, the Federal Bureau of Investigation says, is currently $10,000. The average amount from all reports of missing funds from banks, including bank fraud and embezzlement, according to F.B.I. statistics, is about $19,000. Donn B. Parker, a computer-security expert at Stanford Research Institute (now S.R.I. International), in Menlo Park, California, who has made a specialty of gathering information on computer abuse and is the author of a book called *Crime by Computer,* carried out a study of forty-two computer-related bank frauds and embezzlements committed in this country between 1962 and 1975, and found that the average take per crime was $430,000. While some reported computer crimes involve the theft or embezzlement of only thousands of dollars, quite a few involve very large sums; $1 million from a computer crime is considered a respectable but not an extraordinary score. Still another attraction of crime by computer is the fact that once someone succeeds in breaking the security of a computer system, large amounts of money are not necessarily any more difficult for him to steal or embezzle than small ones. The total sums being stolen or obtained by fraud in this country through the subversion of the computer-processing system are difficult to estimate, but a report on white-collar crime by the U.S. Chamber of Commerce guesses that there may be losses of $100 million or more annually as a result of computer-related crimes. Estimates by other computer-security specialists have been as high as $300 million a year.

2

The Equity Funding Fraud

Ironically, the largest sum known to have been lost through a single computer crime involved not some disloyal company employee embezzling funds but a scheme directed by the company management itself. The victims were the company's customers. The crime in question was an integral part of the great Equity Funding Corporation of America scandal, which broke in 1973. From the mid-1960s until the company's true condition came to light, Equity Funding, which had its headquarters in Los Angeles, was considered one of the hottest stocks on Wall Street. Equity Funding's apparent prosperity was based on the theory that by dealing in both mutual funds and insurance policies the company could make both kinds of investment highly attractive to potential customers; the customers would invest in mutual-fund shares through the company and at the same time buy life insurance issued by the company. Equity Funding itself would then pay the life-insurance premiums, recording the payments as a loan to the customer and using the mutual-fund shares he had bought as collateral for the loan. By this device, the customer was supposed to be able to make good use of cash that he might otherwise have had to tie up in insurance. From 1969 on, the company officer who took complete charge of this apparently successful operation was Stanley Goldblum, the chairman of the board. Under Goldblum's direction, the company embarked on a program of corporate expansion and acquisition. According to the report of Robert M. Loeffler, the trustee in bankruptcy, that program began more and more to depend upon fraud and misrepresentation, the main purpose being to raise the company's profitability illegally and so keep its stock—of which Goldblum and some of his associates in the company were major holders—selling at high prices.

The manner in which this scheme was carried out has caused the Equity Funding case to be characterized by some people, including Loeffler, as a securities fraud and by others as a computer fraud. True, it was only in the last few years of the fraud that the company's computer was brought into use as a tool to further—and further conceal—the plot, but the turn that the Equity Funding fraud took in this phase has the quality of a modern corporate reënactment of Nikolai Gogol's novel *Dead Souls*. Pavel Ivanovitch Tchitchikov, the novel's wily antihero, travels through the heart of Russia making what are represented as authentic purchases of serfs, who are then supposed to be resettled as workers on an estate that Tchitchikov claims to own in a remote part of the country. However, the serfs, although their names are listed in the most recent provincial census, do not exist except in name, having died since the census was compiled. The scheme devised by Tchitchikov—and eventually uncovered—was to acquire these nonexistent people by formal deed, exactly as though they were alive, and to use these deeds as collateral in obtaining a large government mortgage, available only to serf-owners. With this loan in hand, he dreamed, he could proceed to buy real serfs and live prosperously on an estate bought with the government mortgage.

Had Tchitchikov's adventures taken place in the United States in the early 1970s, it could very well have occurred to him, as he considered various opportunities, that one way of converting nonexistent souls into hard cash would be to set himself up in the life-insurance business, use a computer to record insurance policies on people who didn't exist, and then sell the supposedly genuine policies to other insurance companies, through a system of reinsurance which people in the business customarily use in order to spread their actuarial risks and obtain ready cash. That is what several officers in charge of Equity Funding did, as an integral part of a vast securities fraud. In order to raise the price of Equity Funding stock, which by the end of the 1960s had fallen from its spectacular highs, some people in charge of the company began to make wholesale additions to their lists of genuine policyholders, the additions consisting of computerized bogus life-insurance-policy records, which were then sold to reinsurers under an arrangement whereby the reinsurer would bear some or all of the risks involved. The risks turned out to be only too real. The bogus records were manufactured within Equity Funding by a specially assigned staff and were fed into the company's computer as evidence of its growing salable assets.

At first, these records existed only in a computerized summary form—listing, for example, the age, sex, policy number, premium, and coverage for a nonexistent policyholder, along with his invented name. The tapes on which this bogus information was recorded had been compiled from existing tapes that contained basic insurance information on real customers; when the genuine information was transferred, it was doctored by the substitution of fake policy numbers. And when the bogus business was rerouted in its new form into the computer, it was given the special code sign "Department 99" to identify it to the plotters, and to the computer, as requiring special handling when the occasion required. The computer was then used to process the bogus records in an ostensibly normal way, and the bogus policies, represented by computer printouts of doctored information, were sold—along with legitimate policies, belonging to real customers—to reinsurers. Since the terms of the sales gave the reinsurers the right to receive, after one year of the existence of each policy, the premiums supposed to be paid by the policyholder, Equity Funding required cash to cover these expected premium payments. Much of the cash was raised from sales to reinsurers based on yet additional spurious policyholder records, thereby adding to the pyramid.

However, in order to be able to substantiate such bogus computerized records to auditors or reinsurers, where that should become necessary, the conspirators manufactured "original" paper documents on which the fake computerized information was supposedly based. For some time, these records were manufactured by company executives at what the bankruptcy trustee's report called "fraud parties," lasting well into the night, at the opulent company headquarters. At these sessions, some of the computerized records of the nonexistent insured people were modified to make them appear more genuine. For example, to avoid actuarial anomalies that might be noticed by the reinsurers, a certain number of the insured people had to be shown to have died in the course of a given year, and so, at the fraud parties, the conspirators would deprive various nonexistent policyholders of their supposed lives, converting them into truly dead souls. That did not bring the computerized existence of the supposed deceased to an end, however, because after declaring them dead the conspirators would then file with the reinsurers death-benefit claims, which were to be passed on to the heirs of the departed. The money received from the reinsurers on the basis of these bogus claims totaled $1,175,000, most of which was put into Equity Funding's own accounts, and showed up in its books as current earnings. And in a computer fraud within a computer fraud, a smaller sum—$144,000—was routed into the personal bank accounts of particular conspirators, who took this action without the knowledge of the Equity Funding management people directing the original fraud.

In the spring of 1971, the ramifications of the Equity Funding computer swindle grew to such proportions that the conspirators estimated that there would be a requirement that year for between 20,000 and 50,000 bogus files, which, as before, would mostly be doctored variations of existing policyholders' files, with new names and policy numbers added—both in computerized form, for eventual sale to reinsurers, and, in selected samples, in the form of supportive documentation for the company's auditors. After the all-night fraud parties grew too onerous, the bogus computerized information was compiled not at the company headquarters but in a separate office, on Maple Drive, in Beverly Hills. The manual back-up operation to support the fictional computerized lists included the manufacture of fake credit reports and fake medical reports on the nonexistent policyholders. When the auditors examining the computer printouts of the doctored tapes asked Equity Funding officers for the raw documentation on policyholders in the computerized file, the conspirators would obligingly promise to provide such documentation in the form of sample policies chosen by the computer at random. They would then order printouts of the samples, but since all the fake policies were tagged with the Department 99 code, they were able to instruct the computer to exclude all Department 99 records. They would inform the auditors that these particular files were in use at the moment, and would be available the next morning—meanwhile instructing their operatives on Maple Drive to rush them into being.

During 1972, the Equity Funding computer readouts on the files of its fictitious policyholders recorded $14.5 million worth of business—which, of course, had never existed. (In terms of the face value of all the life-insurance policies supposedly in force, Equity Funding claimed it to total, during this period, $3.2 billion. But of this alleged face value, the bankruptcy trustee's report calculated that $2.1 billion was fictitious.) Of a total of 97,000 computer-recorded policies of insured citizens, about 64,000 turned out to be the records of electronic dead souls. All told, the computer-fraud component of the Equity Funding scandal served as a means of furthering a larger fraud, in which, out of $737 million in assets that the company reported in its last financial statement, $185 million was nonexistent. Besides the reinsurers and institutional investors, tens of thousands of genuine insurance policyholders and investors in the mutual-fund operations of Equity Funding were heavily victimized in the whole operation.

The conspiracy fell apart in March of 1973 after a former employee of Equity Funding reported details of it to the New York State Insurance Department and to a Wall Street insurance analyst named Raymond Dirks, who, it seems, in turn notified some of his commercial clients as well as New York Stock Exchange officials of what he had heard. The worth of Equity Funding shares plunged wildly on the New York Stock Exchange. On March 27th, examiners from the California Insurance Department in the Equity Funding premises took firm security measures to guard records there, after notification from the federal Securities and Exchange Commission (based on word from an informer inside the company) that some incriminating computer tapes had been very recently altered and that other tapes were being systematically erased. Goldblum and several other Equity Funding officers were subsequently arrested, tried, and sent to prison on fraud charges.

For all the huge sums involved, the Equity Funding fraud, regarded only in terms of its computer-crime elements, does not seem to have been a particularly sophisticated affair compared with some other frauds, many of them committed on a less grand scale. It was simply a reckless pyramiding operation, which was bound to be uncovered sooner or later, and only surprisingly inadequate auditing procedures and downright gullibility and carelessness on the part of big Wall Street institutional investors permitted it to continue as long as it did. It depended on the use of the computer printout merely as a screen to make the detection of a vast amount of deliberate misinformation more difficult by routine auditing, and did not involve astute manipulation of the internal workings of the computer itself to make the traces of the crime extremely difficult to detect, as do the more adroit examples of computer crime. Since the criminal element directing the fraud consisted of management itself, there was no need to conceal the misuse of the computer from company officials. Furthermore, the fraud was carried out by a fairly extensive internal conspiracy. The more effective computer crimes are seldom the work of such conspiracies, for when the thoughtful computer criminal seeks an accomplice he usually prefers to turn to his computer console or his terminal keyboard.

3

The Union
Dime Embezzlement

However much management may have come to rely on super-efficient data-processing systems, the systems inevitably contain certain imperfections, and it is the knowledge of these imperfections which can bring a gleam of temptation to the eye of a supposedly trustworthy bank employee—especially one who happens to feel that he has been treated unfairly by management. Such feelings encouraged a man I will call Stephen Hattner, the chief teller of the Park Avenue branch of the Union Dime Savings Bank, between 1970 and 1973, to manipulate accounts using a remote terminal at his office so that the bank's computer regularly printed out evidence that the bank's books were in order—which in fact they were, though the accounts themselves weren't. When the fraud was eventually uncovered, in the spring of 1973, it was not because of alertness on the part of the bank management, or because of suspicions held by any of the tellers whom Hattner had been in charge of, or through the supposedly elaborate security safeguards built into the bank's own auditors. Rather, it was because of a police raid on the headquarters of a large bookmaking operation, whose members happened to be the subject of a federal, state, and local investigation.

On the raided premises, police seized a list of the bookies' customers, in which Hattner's name was included. It appeared from the bookie records that Hattner had been a big-spending customer. The police began an investigation in the hope of tracing the source of his funds, and he was followed to his place of employment. It turned out that Hattner, who was forty-one years old, was earning $11,000 a year, and lived, with his wife and children, in a suburban community in New Jersey, in a two-bedroom garden apartment, which he rented for $275 a month. During the years when he had been stealing from the bank, he had been betting as much as $30,000 a day on the races and other sports events, and was a heavy loser. All the money he dropped came out of the bank in cash. He had embezzled more than $1.5 million. None of the money was ever recovered. All of it had been blown, through the bookies, at the race track or on professional basketball. In its place, at the bank, was a set of Union Dime computer printouts that, over the three years of Hattner's criminal activities, indicated that the bank's accounts were in perfect balance.

Basically, what Hattner had done was to exploit his position as chief teller to take advantage of an error-correction routine that was built into Union Dime's computer system. By this means he was able, through a computer terminal he was authorized to use, to modify bank records so that customers who conducted transactions at Union Dime thought they had money in their accounts which they didn't have, and the computer, having been so instructed by Hattner, was moving the phantom sums from account to account in seemingly perfect order. While using the terminal to keep the books neatly in balance, Hattner moved money—or, rather, data representing money—among hundreds of accounts at Union Dime to prevent the discovery of the substantial shortages he was causing. Without any knowledge on the part of his family or his associates, Hattner had been a confirmed gambler for years. Also, he felt that the management was badly overworking and underpaying him.

In 1970, when he began taking money to finance his gambling, one device he used was the looting of accounts in which there was little movement of money. In this he was helped by the fact that Union Dime did not send out monthly statements to its customers. Instead, it issued passbooks to them, and when customers wished to make deposits or withdrawals, or to receive interest on their accounts, they had to appear at the bank with their passbooks. When a teller put a passbook on the carriage of a registering machine connected to the bank's central computer, a transaction was recorded both in the passbook and in the bank's computer system. Hattner developed a special way of treating certain of these transactions. In the first period of his embezzlement, he concentrated on giving his unusual treatment to accounts having large balances—usually of $100,000 or more. At the end of a banking day, he would look over the computer printouts of the day's transactions and pick out any large-balance accounts that had just been opened and recorded in the normal manner in the customer's passbook and in the computer records. If one of the accounts that Hattner picked out showed, for example, a $100,000 deposit, he would sit down at the computer terminal with the account number and, using his authority as chief teller, type out what is known as a supervisor's override—an error-correction instruction—and have the computer change the $100,000-deposit figure to $50,000. (The customer's passbook, of course, would continue to show $100,000.) Hattner would then go into his cash box or the bank vault and pocket $50,000 in cash. Unless the customer made a large withdrawal, the chances that the discrepancy would be discovered immediately were relatively small, Hattner reasoned.

One thing he had to watch out for was interest payments, which were generally made quarterly. When the date for an interest payment approached, Hattner would take the missing principal from another account and move it, through the computer terminal, to the first account. For Union Dime's day-of-deposit accounts, interest was payable on the last day of each quarter of the year, but its time-deposit accounts were payable two days after that. Hattner used the difference in these due dates to transfer money back and forth so that no irreconcilable discrepancies could be detected either by customers or by bank officials.

As Hattner's embezzlement went on, he had to deal with more and more accounts, until, by means of his instructions through the computer terminal, he was juggling money among some fifty accounts at a time. He kept track of the accounts by notes he made on scraps of paper, which he put in his pockets, and as the fraud continued and the complication increased, his pockets became stuffed with these scraps. However, he appears not to have been much worried about the visits of the bank's auditors; he always had advance notice of their arrival, and he said subsequently that when they came he was well prepared and had little difficulty satisfying them. If the auditors asked him to explain an apparent mistake in an account, Hattner would appear concerned, go through the motions of checking on the discrepancy by telephone, and tell the auditors that he had discovered it to be the result of a data-processing error. On the spot, he would type an error-correction instruction into the computer as an ostensible resolution of the discrepancy. Out of sight of the auditors, however, he would further adjust the computer record by moving sums among accounts in such a way that the computer showed the accounts involved to be in balance. When Hattner was on vacation—he was careful never to take long ones—and discrepancies in customer accounts were brought to the attention of other tellers, they left memos for him so that he could resolve the discrepancies on his return. When he got back, he would sit down at the computer terminal and quickly make the necessary adjustments.

As time went on, and as Hattner grew more experienced in embezzlement, he tried to simplify the paperwork of his manipulations—his pockets were overflowing with his notes, and he was hiding slips of paper in his desk—by concentrating on accounts represented by certificates of deposit that were redeemable, with interest, on a certain date. He felt that he could avoid the complications of adjusting the regular accounts every quarter to reflect the usual interest, and concern himself merely with covering up the disappearance of money when particular certificates reached maturity. When that happened, he would calculate the interest due, add it to the principal, and pay the customer in cash, which he would obtain by altering the computer records of some other account.

In carrying out the fraud—particularly in its later period—Hattner, though he evidently felt no sympathy for the bank, became concerned that if he was caught individual depositors whose accounts he had been juggling would suffer financial harm. He knew that some of them were elderly people who had invested their life savings in Union Dime, and, out of a sense of responsibility for their situation, he became increasingly careful to see to it that, after a certain amount of juggling, his net defalcations from individual accounts did not exceed $20,000—the limit for which individual deposits at all banks were then insured by the Federal Deposit Insurance Corporation. When the F.D.I.C. raised the insurance limit to $40,000 per account, Hattner had no hesitation about raising his fraud limit to the same amount per customer. After his crime came to light, all the losses of individual depositors were, in fact, covered by insurance. In a Manhattan court, Hattner, charged with grand larceny to the extent of approximately $1.5 million, pleaded guilty and expressed remorse for his acts. He received a lenient prison sentence of twenty months, of which, with good behavior, he served fifteen. While he was in prison, he acted as a clerk in the assistant warden's office and taught a course in high-school mathematics—with the help, as it happened, of computer-connected instructional terminals. After his release, he found work as a cabdriver in New Jersey. Like the Union Dime management, he prefers not to discuss the case with the press.

One of the unusual aspects of the Union Dime embezzlement, in terms of computer crime, is that Hattner was able to take away his proceeds in the form of hard cash, directly from the till. A further point of interest is that, for all his ability to conceal his computer-terminal fraud from the bank management and the auditors, he had had no training at all in computer science, having been given only enough instruction in how to operate a terminal to carry out his normal work. He had no special knowledge of the internal circuitry and programming of the computer itself. What he was able to learn about beating the system he learned primarily from his experience behind the bank counter—how instructions were typed into the computer and how the output of the computer, in the form of printouts, was modified by this input. That and a certain nimbleness, plus his familiarity with bank routine—and, of course, the pressing needs of his gambling activities—were what enabled him to make away with so much money for so long. If his bookmakers had not indiscreetly kept his name in their files, he might well have kept up his embezzlement for quite a while longer than he did.

4

Electronic Thieves' Market

While there is a growing trend for people who carry out crimes in banking systems to do so by falsifying data they put into the computer from keyboard terminals, some of the more remunerative frauds and thefts have been committed without the criminals actually touching the keys of a terminal or even going near the computer. What the criminals have employed in such cases is a knowledge of the operating system used and the security flaws inherent in it. Some of the devices used to best the computer are engagingly simple—as in the case of a young man who, obviously knowing something about the ways of computers, applied for and received a twelve-month installment loan from a New York bank. On receiving from the bank, together with the loan, the book of computer-coded coupons he was supposed to send in with his monthly payments, he tore out the last payment coupon in the book instead of the first and sent it in to the bank along with one month's payment. He then received a computer-generated letter from the bank thanking him effusively for paying off his loan so promptly and assuring him of his excellent credit standing. The young man didn't exactly *steal* from the bank—he just left it up to the computer to make the next move. The bank involved has since fixed that little programming oversight, and the young man—who claimed he had simply made a mistake—was not prosecuted.

In another example, this one involving the use of a computer as a tool for collusion with an inside source, a man opened a substantial account at a New York bank several years ago. In doing so, he informed an officer of the bank that he manufactured metal furniture on the West Coast. He told the banker that he was about to open a plant in the East, and said he would have his bank on the West Coast transfer a large sum of money into his New York account for that purpose. Soon, as the officer had been led to expect, the sum of $2 million was transferred from the West Coast bank via a computerized system, such as is regularly used to move funds between major banking institutions. But some time later, the transaction was discovered to have been a fraudulent one. The West Coast manufacturing concern was nonexistent, and so was its West Coast bank account. By the time the fraud was discovered, the shadowy manufacturer had taken the $2 million and disappeared. The origin of the fraud came to light after an investigation of the West Coast bank employees who were likely to have typed the instructions for the transfer. Normally, the typing of the orders was done through computer terminals by a staff of four women, of whom three were still employed when the investigation was ordered. The fourth woman was said to have resigned her job recently because of an unhappy love affair.

The woman, when she was sought out and interviewed at home, indicated that she had left her job after being dropped by her boyfriend. Her description of him matched that given by the New York bank for the self-described furniture manufacturer. The woman admitted sending the computer message, but said that she had thought it was a joke. The missing boyfriend, who was evidently familiar with the automatic nature of the transfer of banking funds by computer, had prevailed upon her one day to transmit $2 million to his own East Coast account. He said that he wanted to play a prank on a computer-operator friend of his at the New York end of the line, who would understand that the message was a fake and get a big kick out of it. Since the missing boyfriend, purported depositor, and pseudo-manufacturer was not available for questioning by the police, the two banks involved in the $2 million transfer were left with the computerized message as a souvenir.

Some of the most ingenious computer-aided crimes to date have been pulled off without even the degree of personal interference with the computer exemplified in the case of the phantom manufacturer. A few of these depended on the banks' use of what is called the magnetic-ink character-recognition imprinting system—notably, those blobby-looking numbers that usually appear at the bottom of a bank customer's checks and personal deposit slips, permitting them to be read by computer and automatically sorted and processed. In the Washington, D.C., area some time ago, a new depositor at a bank carried out an almost immaculate computer crime by out-thinking the bank on the convenience offered by the magnetic-ink character-recognition system. The method was close to simplicity itself. According to one record of the affair, the depositor opened a new account in the normal way and made a deposit of several thousand dollars, to show himself a man of some substance. And, in the normal way, he received from the bank his personal checks and deposit slips, both bearing at the bottom left, in magnetic-ink computer-readable code, his account number. The slips, however, he did not use. Instead, the depositor visited the bank and went to the desk where customers bringing money or checks in for deposit filled out their deposit slips. For the convenience of customers who had forgotten to bring their own deposit slips, the bank provided stacks of blank slips in trays under the desk. The new depositor picked up a hefty batch of these blank deposit slips, but he did not fill them out. Instead, he took them to premises where a typewriter equipped to write in magnetic-ink characters was available. Using this special typewriter, he imprinted his account number in magnetic ink at the bottom of the blank deposit forms. He then returned to the bank on different occasions and added these magnetically-printed forms to the neat pile of blank deposit slips in the trays. Then he went away and waited for the jackpot.

Other customers streamed into the bank and, dipping into the trays of deposit slips, innocently recorded their own deposits in the usual way. After the deposits and the deposit slips were routinely accepted by tellers, the deposit slips disappeared into the maw of the bank's computer-actuated sorters. The deposit slips that bore no magnetic-ink account numbers were sorted out by the machine for manual handling, and those that did bear magnetic-ink identification were automatically routed for deposit in the accounts represented by the magnetic code. In this way, the computer funneled the deposits of scores of the bank's customers into the new depositor's account. And by the time the customers began to complain that checks they were issuing against their deposits were bouncing, the new depositor, to whose account other depositors had miraculously added a quarter of a million dollars, had drawn out a hundred thousand of it and disappeared. A similar scheme, also involving the embezzlement of a large sum of money, was carried out in a New York bank several years ago, and, on a smaller scale, the same stunt was pulled on a Boston bank.

An even craftier scheme, this one rather more elaborate than the Washington swindle, also revolved around the use of falsified magnetic-ink characters on checks to confound and defeat the computerized banking system. As in the cases of the other magnetic-code frauds, this one was carried out without anyone's ever laying a finger on the computer itself or any of its keyboard terminals. The fraud began with a new customer opening an account at a New York bank with a substantial amount of money. He received his coded checks and deposit slips from the bank, and he used the coded deposit slips in the usual way—without transforming the deposit-slip desk at his bank into a sort of financial cuckoo's nest, as the Washington-area depositor did. Going one step further than the Washington man, the New York man sought out a knowledgeable, and willing, printer, and what he then did was to have some new checks printed on blank-check forms similar to those used by his new bank. With one exception, the printed checks bore the same information as the originals, including the depositor's name and address and name and address of the bank. The exception was the set of magnetic characters in the lower-left corner of the checks. There the depositor had printed, in magnetic ink, a set of numbers different from the set the bank had assigned him.

The manner in which these numbers was changed was the key to the scheme. The magnetic-ink account numbers used by banks are preceded by a three-digit code, also in magnetic ink, indicating the bank where the account is registered. These three digits inform a computer at a Federal Reserve System bank—through which checks are routed between most banks for clearance—what bank the check is to be returned to so that the transaction can be completed. Suppose, purely for the purpose of illustration, that the computer criminal opening the big account in a New York bank did so at the bank I happen to use, which is the Chemical Bank. In changing the magnetic-ink account number, the depositor altered the original account number to one that contained the wrong number of digits. At the same time, he altered the initial three digits to those belonging to a real bank on the West Coast—let us say, again purely for the purpose of illustration, the Bank of America in Los Angeles. He then began opening accounts at other banks, making deposits in these accounts in the form of the altered checks bearing his printed name and the printed name of the Chemical Bank—along with the magnetic code for the Bank of America. These checks were accepted for deposit subject to clearance.

From one of the banks involved, such a check was sent to a Federal Reserve bank for routing to the bank of origin. Although the check bore the name and address of the Chemical Bank in New York, the Federal Reserve data-processing system scanned only the magnetic-ink code on it, identified it as a Bank of America check, and routed it to Los Angeles. The check remained in transit for perhaps two days. At the end of that time, it was run through the computer mechanism at the Bank of America. The computer, instantly searching its memory for a Bank of America account number matching that of the magnetic-ink strip on the check, rejected the check, which then went into a clerical pool for manual handling. Since the printed logotype on the check clearly identified it as a check that belonged in the Chemical Bank in New York, the clerk handling the machine-rejected check sent it back to the Chemical Bank by mail, assuming that a simple routing error had been made. The check was then in transit for another two days. Back at the Chemical Bank, the check was put into the computerized sorting system for final clearance. But instead of that, it went into motion again: the Chemical Bank computing system passed it on to the Federal Reserve System, which routed it out to the Los Angeles bank again, which routinely sent it back to New York, and so on.

In the meantime, other large checks from the same depositor were making the rounds in the same way. Because they were not rejected by the Chemical Bank, they were assumed by the corresponding bank to be good. The fraud was uncovered only when checks issued by the depositor became so frayed from mechanical handling in the computer system that they could no longer be read automatically; a clerk in one of the corresponding banks then noticed the discrepancy between the name of the bank as it appeared in plain print on one of the checks and the magnetic-ink numerical code designation. By that time, according to an auditor who told me of the affair, the depositor had disappeared with more than $1 million in cash.

It seems clear to anyone looking over press reports and other accounts of computer crimes that many of the crimes are variations on certain basic techniques. Yet one cannot help being impressed by the sheer diversity of the efforts. For example, the technique employed by Hattner at Union Dime to juggle accounts around in the computer appears in less spectacular but no less ingenious variations in a number of other computer crimes. One such type of computer embezzlement involves the use of what Donn Parker refers to as the salami, or thin-slice-at-a-time, technique—reliance on tiny increments, sometimes literally only a fraction of a penny at a time. The criminal programs the computer to divert these minute sums to his own account from a number of accounts or transactions, and then patiently lies in wait to collect the steadily growing fruit of his mini-embezzlements. One way in which computer criminals might employ the salami technique is to round down any sums ending in fractions to the nearest whole number—for example, fractions of pennies as these are computed in interest-bearing accounts. In the meantime, the criminal has established a dummy account at the same bank, and he programs the computer to divert the surplus from the round-downs to this account. Quietly accumulating year in and year out, these fractional sums can mount handsomely, and usually neither the bank nor the depositors know what is going on. Even when the bank does suspect jiggery-pokery, it may not do much about it. The cost and effort involved in tracing and prosecuting any impropriety would be considerably greater than the sums involved.

Parker told me that he felt he had almost certain knowledge of one salami-style embezzlement that was still being carried out at a bank whose officers he had talked with. The embezzler, he said, was evidently using the bank's computer to transfer twenty or thirty cents at a time, at random, from 300 checking accounts at the bank and diverting the money to a dummy account for his own use. The computer criminal was careful never to divert sums from any particular account more often than three times a year. Because a customer was unlikely to notice such a small discrepancy in his monthly bank statement—or, if he did notice it, to find it worth his while to go to the bank and argue over it—the embezzlement was likely to go on and on. Parker suspects that many thousands of bank customers are being fleeced regularly of small sums in this fashion in cities throughout the country, since these people trust the accuracy of the computerized statements, and if there is a small discrepancy they are apt to put it down to their own poor arithmetic.

In another variation of the salami technique, two programmers who were employed by a big New York garment firm instructed the company's computer to increase by two cents the amount withheld from their fellow-employees' paychecks each week for federal taxes. They further programmed the computer to direct the two cents per employee per week to their own federal withholding accounts. The result was that at the end of the year they received the money in the form of refund checks from the Internal Revenue Service, which had been acting as an unwitting bagman for the embezzled sums.

In yet another ingenious variation, a programmer working at a mail-order sales company had its computer round down odd cents in the company's sales-commission accounts and channel the round-downs into a dummy sales-commission account he had established under the name of Zwana. He had invented the name Zwana because he knew that the computer processed the company's accounts in alphabetical order, and he could easily program the computer to transfer all the round-downs into the last account in the computing sequence. The system worked perfectly for three years, and then it failed—not because of a logical error on the culprit's part but because the company, as a public-relations exercise, decided to single out the holders of the first and last sales-commission accounts on its alphabetical list for ceremonial treatment. Thus Zwana was unmasked, and his creator fired.

Computer crime does not necessarily involve the direct theft of money. The near-universal use of electronic data processing in accounting systems has made computer programs that record and control the flow of inventories increasingly subject to manipulations whereby the computer is directed to move goods into criminal hands. The records of thefts or suspected thefts of goods by computer-data manipulation include the physical disappearance, in the early 1970s, of 217 railroad boxcars owned by the bankrupt Penn Central Railroad. The deputy chief of a federal crime force investigating the case concluded that a computer program used by Penn Central to direct the assembly and routing of the company's boxcars had been manipulated to divert the boxcars—which were worth millions of dollars—from Penn Central sidings. F.B.I. agents eventually found them, freshly painted and with the Penn Central markings obscured, on the sidings of the tiny La Salle & Bureau County Railway, in Illinois, which has only fifteen miles of track. The boxcars had apparently been rerouted, with the help of someone who could modify the Penn Central computer input, so that some remarkably sophisticated criminal group could arrange their eventual resale or rental to another railroad system.

According to Lindsay L. Baird, Jr., an independent computer-security consultant, who tries to help large corporations and banks make their data-processing systems tamperproof—or as nearly so as possible—the kind of manipulation that seemed to be responsible for the disappearance of the Penn Central boxcars has also been used to misdirect government supplies of one kind or another into criminal channels. Baird has cited a fraud pulled off in South Korea in the early 1970s, in which, through manipulation of a United States Army supply-computing program largely operated by Korean technicians, huge quantities of food, uniforms, vehicles, gasoline, and other American supplies were diverted into the hands of a Korean gang for resale. Baird, who participated as an Army provost marshal in an investigation of the Korean affair, told me recently that the swindle was so effective that the theft of about $18 million worth of equipment a year was being concealed by the misuse of inventory-and-supply computer programs.

In 1975, in Linden, New Jersey, it was discovered—after the arrest of three men, including a computer-console operator for the Exxon Corporation—that, through the manipulation of an Exxon computer in which records of oil transfers were supposedly kept current, and the alteration of oil gauges, conspirators had been able, in the course of seven years, to make off with about $20 million worth of Exxon fuel. The fuel allegedly had been siphoned from the company's huge Linden refinery into a barge owned by the conspirators. In the first three months of 1975 alone, according to the Union County prosecutor, Exxon lost 1.5 million gallons of fuel, worth half a million dollars.

A fourth example of crime involving the physical diversion and theft of supplies by the use of computers is the case of a young man named Jerry Neal Schneider, who was arrested in Los Angeles in 1972 and charged with stealing what police estimated as $1 million worth of electronic equipment from the Pacific Telephone & Telegraph Company, by means of rigged computer instructions. Schneider, who was twenty-one years old, had been keenly interested in computers for some time. When he was a high-school student, in Los Angeles, his walk to and from school had taken him past a Pacific Telephone supply storeroom, and he had noticed trash cans outside holding papers of various sorts. Schneider, feeling that rummaging through the trash cans might be, as he later recalled, "kind of a fun thing," did so now and then. Sometimes he would find odds and ends of discarded telephone-company equipment and take it home with him. He also began to take home and read discarded copies of telephone-company operating guides. At the time, most of them were nearly meaningless to Schneider, but he held on to them, and gradually built up something of a technical library, of which these guides and other manuals were a part. Eventually, he said, he added to his library, from the trash cans, management guides dealing with how Pacific Telephone ordered equipment from the Western Electric Company. According to Schneider, the guides also "described the methods through which... equipment was ordered to a field-supply location" of Pacific Telephone.

A few years later, Schneider, by then an engineering student at the University of California at Los Angeles, reread the guides and other telephone-company technical publications. It occurred to him then that he had in his possession the key to obtaining a lot of money, and he decided to use it. The details of how he set about doing so are not easy to determine, because Schneider has given differing versions of his actions to different interviewers. But even taking the discrepancies into account, one can form a fairly clear picture of his procedure. What Schneider was after was a system that would enable him to safely order by telephone and then sell expensive equipment purchased by Pacific Telephone. In the material he had found in the trash cans, the company had described the fundamentals of its equipment-ordering system, which was programmed into an I.B.M. 360 computer. Within the Pacific Telephone organization, equipment for installers and repairmen was ordered by phone through computers and delivered to convenient locations by truck in the middle of the night. To place such an order, an employee had to use a series of codes. He needed, among other information, an identification code number designating the site from which the order was coming and an account code number. Schneider, by various ruses—including calls in which he impersonated telephone-company employees, and a visit to telephone-company facilities in which he passed himself off as a free-lance writer preparing a technical article on computerized warehouse systems—pieced together most of the information on codes and procedures necessary for placing unauthorized orders.

Next, he bought an automatic dialer so that his Touch-Tone telephone's signals would resemble those from the equipment used by the authorized employees. In June 1971, after several trial runs, he put into the computer an order for $30,000 worth of telephone equipment, to be delivered to a company drop-off point he had chosen. The order was automatically registered on a punch card and processed by the I.B.M. computer, and the equipment was duly delivered on the designated night. Schneider hauled it away and ordered more. Soon he had formed a corporation grandiosely called the Los Angeles Telephone & Telegraph Company, through which he sold the stolen equipment to private suppliers and users of such apparatus. He continued, month after month, to order equipment without incident. He later said that he once had a $25,000 switchboard delivered to a telephone-company manhole at two o'clock in the morning. The equipment was picked up by a van that looked like a Pacific Telephone van but was a secondhand job bought at auction.

After a while, Schneider had ten people working for his company, and a 6,000-square-foot warehouse, in which he stored the stolen equipment. In January 1972, he was undone by an employee to whom he had refused a salary raise. The disgruntled employee went to the police, the warehouse was raided, and Schneider was arrested. He was charged with grand theft. After some plea bargaining and a promise to coöperate with the police, Schneider was sentenced to sixty days at a prison farm. With time off for good behavior, he served forty days. Of the million dollars' worth of equipment that the police said Schneider had stolen, the prosecution could prove only that he had handled some $5,000 worth. He was able to settle a $250,000 civil suit brought against him by Pacific Telephone for $8,500. After his sojourn at the prison farm, Schneider set himself up in business as a computer-security consultant to various corporations, offering them an insider's knowledge of how to prevent computer crime. The $8,500 that Schneider was obliged to pay Pacific Telephone was far more than offset when, as a result of the publicity surrounding the case, he reportedly was able to sell the story of his computer depredations to a movie company for a substantial sum.

It is perhaps an indication of the degree to which the computer has become a vital element of our society that sets of electronic signals stored in computers have in themselves become entities of great value and the targets of numerous attempts at theft. Most thefts of computer tapes are probably not reported to the police, because the victimized owners prefer to arrange for the tapes' return through private negotiations with the thieves—negotiations that in some cases may involve the passing of money and in others assurances that no prosecution will be undertaken. Sometimes such thefts are unremunerative. According to an item that appeared in the weekly *Computerworld* in 1971, thieves operating at the Los Angeles International Airport stole an air shipment from the Bank of America which included two reels of the bank's computer tapes. The thieves assumed that the tapes contained valuable records and demanded ransom, threatening to destroy them if it was not paid. The ransom attempt failed, because the bank had in its files duplicates of the stolen tapes.

Another attempt at ransoming stolen tapes, which did take into account the existence of backup records, occurred in January 1977 in Europe. According to Interpol, the international police information clearing house, a chief programmer in the computer department of the Rotterdam facilities of Imperial Chemical Industries, Ltd., was accused of absconding with computer-tape records relating to the company's extensive European operations—including a duplicate set of tapes that had been stored in a separate and supposedly secure facility. The programmer allegedly attempted to extort 200,000 pounds in cash from the company for their return. But the ransom scheme failed when, at a rendezvous in Oxford Street in London, the tapes were about to be traded for the ransom, which had been brought to the scene in ten-pound notes by an Imperial Chemical Industries representative. Scotland Yard men, alerted by the company, were lying in wait. On the spot they arrested the programmer and an alleged accomplice, retrieving the missing tapes as well as retaining the ransom money.

However, another attempt in 1973 at computer-tape hijacking, in West Germany, was more successful. In this affair, a computer operator formerly employed by a German corporation reportedly broke into the computer center the corporation used and made off with twenty-two reels of computer tape containing vital information about the company's marketing plans and programs. He reportedly then demanded that the company pay $200,000 for their return. The company had no duplicates of the stolen tapes, and the cost of reconstructing the data would have been greater than the ransom demanded, so the company quietly paid up.

Sometimes electronic penetration of data in a computer system is attempted by a company's competitors, and when it is successful the rewards can be high. An independent computer-security consultant told me not long ago of what appears to be one such case. It concerned prospecting information obtained by a huge oil company that was one of the principal bidders on oil-drilling rights to tracts of government land on the North Slope of Alaska. According to the account I was given, the oil company sent reports from its geologists exploring the field to a central communications post in the area. From a keyboard terminal there, the geological data were sent thousands of miles by telephone line to a computer at the offices of the oil company. Later on, after the data had been transmitted to the computer, the same remote terminal received from the company headquarters financial analyses based on the geological data. The analyses indicated the sums that the company's representatives in Alaska might bid for the drilling rights. After the company lost to its competitors by a suspiciously narrow margin on most of the bids it submitted, it began an investigation into the security of the reporting system. The investigation concluded that someone using very inexpensive rented electronic equipment and representing the interests of the competitors had tapped the oil company's computer communication line, printed out the data, and used the information to the advantage of the competitors. The sums at stake probably ran into scores of millions of dollars.

Not only does a lot of the information in a computer have great value but the programs themselves—the step-by-step instructions incorporated into the computer's memory to direct the complex processing of data—are considered valuable assets by their designers and owners. Designing a computer program for the handling of specific kinds of data can be a tedious and time-consuming affair, often involving the ingenious application of computer logic. Computer programs have therefore been the targets of numerous outside attempts—usually made on behalf of competitors—to pry them loose from the computer's memory and have them duplicated for gainful purposes. This form of industrial espionage or thievery goes on between manufacturing and other corporations possessing their own computers and also between corporations whose business it is to supply other companies with computer-processing services on a time-sharing basis.

One such case involved a man I will call Eli Bart, a young man who was considered the best computer programmer on the staff of a California computer-service company known as the University Computing Company, or U.C.C., in Palo Alto. In 1971, according to court records, Bart masterminded the theft—actually carried out by a computer from a computer—of a program that had been developed by a competing company called Information Systems Design, Inc., or I.S.D., of Oakland. The services provided by both organizations involved the design as well as the processing of computer programs for their customers. As it happened, the two companies were competing to provide specialized services for, among other corporate customers, the Shell Development Corporation, in Emeryville, and Aerojet-General, in Sacramento. U.C.C. was by far the bigger of the two computer-service companies; its sales were about $100 million a year, while those of I.S.D. were about $1 million. However, there was one technical area in which the I.S.D. people considered themselves ahead. That was the application of a computer program designed by I.S.D. which made it possible for the company to provide its clients, at their remote sites, with visual engineering information on calculations made by the service company's computer. The I.S.D. people believed that in the design of this special program, which they called PLOT/TRANS, they had a device that would eliminate the need for certain expensive equipment required for complete two-way instant computing services involving graphics between customers' facilities and I.S.D. To this extent, U.C.C., which did not have any such system worked out, was at a competitive disadvantage.

Bart decided to improve his company's position by raiding the memory bank of the I.S.D. computer and getting the secret of its PLOT/TRANS program. (The program itself had not cost I.S.D. very much to develop—possibly about $5,000 worth of time—but the I.S.D. people put its potential value to the company at $1 million or more.) Bart set about penetrating the I.S.D. computer from a telephone-connected terminal at U.C.C. headquarters. To communicate with the I.S.D. computer, he needed three separate informational keys: the unlisted telephone number of the I.S.D. computer; a number designating the authorized terminal site from which he was calling; and an account number identifying the caller, for billing purposes. Bart was able to obtain the unlisted telephone number by visiting the offices of Shell Development, which was, after all, a client of U.C.C. as well as of I.S.D. And because of this double connection he already knew the identifying site and account numbers of Shell, as both I.S.D. and U.C.C. had, as a convenience to Shell, given it the same identification numbers for access to their computers. Naturally, Bart also needed the identifying name of the program he sought, and this he received from an acquaintance at Aerojet-General, which was a PLOT/TRANS user.

There was a certain hitch to this plan, since the form of data flow at the keyboard terminal employed by Bart did not precisely match that used at the Shell Development terminal site, which was a Univac 1004. However, on January 19, 1971, when Bart attempted access to the I.S.D. computer he was able to manipulate his entry communications to make it appear that his instructions were from the Univac used by Shell. Once he had successfully gained access to the I.S.D. computer by means of his identifying codes, he fed it instructions to send out a set of signals that would allow his computer to duplicate the PLOT/TRANS program on punch cards. This attempt failed, because Bart didn't know that the I.S.D. computer—unlike U.C.C.'s—lacked the capability to punch out cards at a remote terminal. When nothing happened, Bart gave it a command to take a table of contents of the PLOT/TRANS file and asked it to list the symbolic information in that file. This time, the I.S.D. computer responded, and the result was a high-speed printout, on the raider's computer, of the PLOT/TRANS program.

The printout took three seconds. In his delight at successfully snatching the program from his competitor's computer, Bart did not consider the possibility that the I.S.D. computer might have responded to his initial, apparently unsuccessful, instruction without his knowing it. But this was what had happened. The I.S.D. computer *had* complied with Bart's instruction to punch out a set of cards representing the PLOT/TRANS program. Since the cards were identified by the I.S.D. computer as having been requested by Shell Development, they were routinely delivered to that company, but nobody there could recall asking for them. An I.S.D. employee visiting Shell Development a few days later recognized the cards as representing an I.S.D. program. Computer records at Shell confirmed that no request for the program had been made. Suspicious about what was going on, the I.S.D. people had the origin of the requesting call to the I.S.D. computer traced, and that led to U.C.C. and to Bart.

On February 19, 1971, police, accompanied by an I.S.D. computer-programming specialist and armed with a search warrant, raided the U.C.C. premises. The action had a novel legal feature, in that it was apparently the first time a warrant included specific authority to search the memory system of a computer for evidence of a crime. During the search, which took some nine hours, all the information stored in the computer's memory devices was read out onto tapes, which the police impounded. In Bart's office, the searchers uncovered handwritten notes on how the I.S.D. computer might be penetrated, and also uncovered a computer printout of the stolen I.S.D. program. Bart was charged with the theft of a trade secret, eventually pleaded guilty, and was fined $5,000 and placed on three years' probation. As a result of a civil suit brought against U.C.C. for engaging in unfair competition, a jury awarded I.S.D. $300,000 in punitive and compensatory damages.

Another computer misuse, and a fairly frequent one, consists in gaining unauthorized entry into a computer to make free use of its data-processing facilities. In one case, which was reported in the Los Angeles *Times* in December 1975, a computer-service organization called Manufacturing Data Systems, Inc., of Ann Arbor, Michigan, was the victim. According to the report, a former employee of M.D.S.I., who was currently employed by a North Hollywood firm, the W. & R. Tool and Manufacturing Company, was charged in Los Angeles with grand theft of computer time for using secret terminal passwords assigned to English and French representatives of M.D.S.I., in order to gain access to the company's computer by long-distance telephone and use it to produce, in Hollywood, a numerically punched tape that was then used to direct the operation of computer-connected tool-manufacturing machines owned by W. & R. Tool. The total amount of computer time consumed in the penetration was 143 hours, with a commercial value of $15,000. Other cases involving theft of computer time range from that of a big Midwestern bookmaker who obtained surreptitious entry into the computer of a university to make his betting calculations to that of a high-school student, an electronics enthusiast, who found in a trash basket the password assigned to an analyst employed by a computer-service company, obtained further information on the logical structure of the service company's computer system, and then used great amounts of computer time to play computer games.

The theft and unauthorized sale of computerized information, in printouts or other forms, appear to have become widespread in the computer industry, and many instances of such illegal trafficking are on record. A number of them concern unauthorized printouts and the sale of lists of one sort or another that are recorded in computer systems. For example, several years ago three computer operators were alleged to have extracted from an Encyclopaedia Britannica computerized list and sold nearly three million customer names; the list was valued by the publisher at $1 million. In 1973, a computer operator employed at the Illinois Driver Registration Bureau, who had been bribed with $10,000 by outsiders, stole a tape reel of drivers' names and addresses which had a direct-mail value of $70,000, and the stolen list was put to commercial use. In a variation of this scheme, employees of the New York Department of Motor Vehicles were charged in 1974 with adding more than 1,000 names to computer printouts of lists of approved applicants for drivers' licenses. These names belonged mostly to recent non-English-speaking immigrants who had never had the required eye examinations or taken the necessary written and road tests, but licenses for these people were automatically issued on the basis of the computer printouts. Working in league with a private driving school, the officials responsible collected between $200 and $400 for each license thus authorized by the computer. The scheme netted about a third of a million dollars.

To unscrupulous computer employees, all sorts of computerized lists have market value. A computer specialist employed by the Australian Taxation Commission is reported to have sold to people with income-tax forms to fill out copies of documentation, based on highly confidential computer logic, that described the computerized methods used by the commission to check on the legitimacy of taxpayers' claims for deductions. With this information as a guide, the taxpayers could safely exaggerate claims for tax deductions. Computer programmers handling payroll accounts have been known to manipulate the data input of parts of payroll lists to give certain employees, for a fee, unauthorized salary raises. Police officers have been accused of selling computerized information concerning criminal records for the use of potential employers: in one case, according to a 1974 report in *Computerworld,* a Massachusetts state-police officer was accused of selling computerized police records to a private detective agency, which then allegedly sold the information to retail stores looking over prospective employees. (At the trial, however, the judge found the officer not guilty on grounds of insufficient evidence.) And in

Chicago in 1971 a police officer was indicted by a federal grand jury on charges of programming the F.B.I. National Crime Information Center computer to obtain information for private use. In Norway, a computer operator employed by the government health service sold records of people with certain ailments. The patients could then be individually approached by a commercial drug-marketing organization.

Computerized voting lists have sometimes been the object of illegal manipulation. In 1971, a computer-service company was accused, in a civil suit brought by the State of California, of using for commercial purposes a computer tape bearing a list of registered voters. The case was settled out of court. In New York City in 1972, a computer operator employed by the Board of Elections was charged with participating in a vote-fraud conspiracy by illegally feeding into a computerized list of registered voters a hundred punch cards containing the names of unregistered voters. In August of 1973, the syndicated columnist Jack Anderson charged that there was "compelling evidence" that some congressmen were misusing the voting computer in the House of Representatives. The computer is activated when a member inserts his personal card in a terminal on the House floor, and it registers both his presence and his yea or nay on a particular vote. Anderson charged that, in violation of House rules against proxy votes, some congressmen, and even pages, had been seen inserting more than one card in the computer, presumably on behalf of absent House members. And in Sweden two employees at a private data center in Helsingborg surreptitiously borrowed computer tapes compiled by the Swedish census bureau and sold the information on them to assorted customers. One customer for the bootlegged tapes was a political party, which bought information on 210,000 voters in a primary election. The thieves were caught when the original tapes were requested for a special computer run and found to be missing.

The functioning of a great part of the modern credit economy revolves around the operation of huge centralized data banks in which computerized information concerning the financial records of consumers and business firms is collected, stored, and sold to clients through commercial credit-reporting networks. So crucial have satisfactory credit ratings become to businessmen and ordinary consumers alike that an underground market in the doctoring of unfavorable credit information has grown and flourished. This situation has proved to offer profitable opportunities to some computer programmers and operators employed by large credit-reporting companies, and also to various people who, although they themselves do not directly handle computers, are knowledgeable enough to beat the computerized credit-reporting system. The largest of the computerized credit-reporting agencies is TRW Credit Data, which is operated by a unit of TRW, Inc., the electronics conglomerate. TRW Credit Data maintains computerized credit files on some 50 million American consumers and provides information on their credit histories to subscribing businesses, such as banks, credit-card companies, oil companies, and retail stores. The data-processing headquarters of TRW Credit Data, in Anaheim, California, seem to have been victimized over a period of years by various well-organized attempts to doctor computerized credit records. An article in the *Wall Street Journal* reported that a federal grand jury in Los Angeles charged in an indictment that a credit-fraud ring had employed a TRW Credit Data employee to alter the credit records on several hundred people who were poor credit risks so as to show them to have excellent credit performance; for this service, fees of between $300 and $1,500 were said to have been charged by the ring for each credit record improved. On the basis of these doctored credit records, poor-risk applicants were able to get loans from banks and savings-and-loan associations, to get credit cards from American Express and Master Charge, and to make credit purchases at department stores and other retail businesses. The scheme was said to have been carried out between August 1974 and March 1975.

Previously, TRW Credit Data, along with other large credit-reporting agencies, had apparently been victimized by members of another criminal gang, who prepared their ground thoroughly in order to create spurious favorable credit reports. Between 1973 and 1974, according to an earlier article in the *Wall Street Journal,* another credit-faking gang went about its business by using as a front a fraudulent business school specializing in credit-reporting procedures. This "school" turned out "graduates" who, with the bogus credentials supplied them, were able, according to California police, to find employment in nationally known mail-order houses, banks, and savings-and-loan associations that all subscribed to TRW Credit Data. As subscribers, such businesses were required to supply computerized credit information on their own customers to TRW Credit Data. This is what the "graduates" did, but much of what they fed into the TRW computer consisted of doctored information that turned poor credit risks into excellent credit prospects. TRW Credit Data, in turn, fed this information on request to other client businesses, to whom bad-risk customers, in league with the gang, had applied for loans and credit. As a result of these manipulations, a number of businesses were said to have suffered large losses on uncollectible loans and other bad debts.

In a reverse form of this sort of computer abuse, the F.B.I. itself, between 1968 and 1972, was the perpetrator of a number of highly improper acts involving computerized information. According to the results of an investigation subsequently undertaken by the Department of Justice, the bureau planted in the files of credit-reporting agencies false adverse information on radicals and other people whose political views were anathema to the bureau—the idea being to harass those citizens by making it difficult, if not impossible, for them to obtain loans or other forms of credit.

As if all the losses through theft and fraud were not enough, organizations using computers must also contend with the acts of irate employees. The cost of identifying and reconstructing information that has been destroyed is often enormous, and disgruntled computer programmers, operators, and clerks are well aware of the serious blows they can strike against their employers by destroying or deliberately altering data within a system. For example, several years ago, at the headquarters of the Yale Express System, Inc., a trucking firm in New York, an overworked computer operator was reported to have taken home with him billing data he was unable to enter into the system by the end of a working day and simply destroyed them. The billing represented in the destroyed data totaled $2 million. And in New York some time ago an annoyed computer-room employee of the Irving Trust Company was said to have attacked with a sharp instrument the computer tapes of all General Electric dividend accounts being processed in the Irving Trust computers at the time, rendering all the data stored on them unusable.

Belden Menkus, an independent computer-security consultant, told me of an act of sabotage with particularly expensive consequences that evidently occurred within the computer staff of a large insurance company in Hartford. According to his account, which has been confirmed by several other computer-security people, the incident involved a woman who was a computer-tape librarian at the company headquarters and was having love affairs with two men in the data-processing division. Apparently, these affairs caused so much turmoil and friction, not only among the principals but within the computer staff generally, that after various scenes and confrontations the tape librarian was told by her supervisor to seek employment elsewhere, and was given thirty days' notice. Before she left, she found a telling way of expressing her opinion of the insurance company. As computer tapes containing data vital to the company came into the tape library, she either erased them or mislabeled and misfiled them. She similarly erased or mislabeled tapes that duplicated the missing data. The damage was not discovered until the day after the librarian left. The company's computer system was thrown into almost complete chaos, and, according to Menkus, "it cost the insurance company ten million dollars to re-create the data this woman had destroyed." For its own reasons the insurance company decided not to prosecute the offender, who, in any case, was obviously unable to repay the $10 million.

If one report is to be believed, even as relentlessly optimistic an organization as the Girl Scouts of the U.S.A. appears not to be immune to resentment in the computer room. According to Donn Parker's records, a disgruntled employee at Girl Scout National Headquarters, in New York, a few years ago expressed her feelings by erasing information on several reels of tape in the computer room, which she accomplished by running a magnet over the reeled tape through flange openings in the sides of the reels.

A French programmer who was dismissed from his job several years ago devised a different scheme for expressing his annoyance with his employer. According to an item in the computer trade publication *Data Management,* the computer program that the employee had been working on at the time of his dismissal was one that would keep his employer's records systematically updated on an annual basis. When he was given notice, he added an instruction to the computer (which, like other systems, has an electronic clock built into its workings) to erase all the company's records as of two years after he departed. Other programmers faced with dismissal have contented themselves with entering instructions into the computer to give them large severance payments or to have their names put on their corporations' pension lists.

Not too surprisingly, the cash-dispensing machines used by banks to provide their customers with cash in remote spots have attracted the attentions of people engaged in computer crimes. Supposedly, these automatic dispensing systems are secure. To get cash from them, a customer must insert his bank credit card in the dispenser and punch out on the machine keyboard a special number assigned to him, along with the sum he wishes to withdraw. The machine then feeds this information into a central computer, which checks it against the customer's correct number and his bank balance or credit balance. If the card is a forgery or is otherwise invalid, the machine clamps down and retains it; if the central computer indicates that the customer has the right identification and the necessary funds in the bank, the machine dispenses the cash—always a limited amount, usually $50 to $100—while the computer deducts the withdrawal from the customer's account. The number of withdrawals that the computer allows a customer in any one day is also limited. However, I have been assured by one security man that there are cases in which cash-dispensing machines have been made to give up sums of money to unauthorized users. Another independent computer-security consultant told me recently that he was in the process of proposing to one large bank a test of its automatic cash-dispensing system, because he was convinced that he could outwit the system and withdraw funds unsecured by his bank account.

A newsletter put out by a British data-security organization reported in December 1974 that a French electronics engineer had been convicted in Tours on a charge of fraudulently obtaining 60,000 francs from bank cash-dispensing machines in four French cities. What the engineer had done, it seems, was to telephone bank-card customers and, identifying himself as a bank official, tell them that the bank, for security reasons, was giving them a new secret number for use at its cash-dispensing terminals; he also asked them, in an apparently routine manner, what their present number was. In every case, he got the number. He then used the secret numbers together with falsified bank cards to get cash from dispensers. He was caught when a dispenser became blocked by one of his cards and he made the mistake of going to the same place the next day to try again.

In Tokyo, in 1974, a kidnapper chose a bank cash-dispensing-machine system as a means of collecting ransom. To prepare the ground for the actual kidnapping, the criminal opened a bank account under the false name of S. Kobayashi, with a false address. He then began to withdraw small sums from among the 348 cash-dispensing machines the bank maintained around Japan, and by making telephone calls to the bank after doing so he was able to calculate that it took the bank's central computer about twenty minutes after the actual dispensing of the cash to determine which dispenser a particular withdrawal had been made from. Some time later, he carried out the kidnapping he had been planning, and he immediately telephoned a demand that the ransom money of 5 million yen—$16,500—in cash be paid into his account. The kidnapper would collect the ransom when he inserted a bank card bearing the name S. Kobayashi in any one of the bank's cash-dispensing machines. By this means, he reasoned, he would be assured of at least twenty minutes of getaway time after he received the ransom money. His scheme failed, however, because as soon as the bank received his demand its data specialists were able to reprogram the bank's central computer to identify instantly the machine in which S. Kobayashi's card would be inserted. The police stationed radio-equipped men within reach of the bank's cash dispensers, and the criminal was caught as he walked away from one of the machines.

5

Frail Auditors,
Frustrated Prosecutors

It is almost universally conceded in the electronic data-processing industry that, even with the help of auditing teams, it is extremely difficult to detect acts of embezzlement, fraud, or thievery in which computers, or the processing routines employed in their operation, are used as the principal tools of crime. It seems to be also agreed that the number of undetected computer-related crimes is probably far greater than the number of those on record. Of course, a considerable amount of fraud occurs under manual accounting systems, and the computer unquestionably offers, through its instant and wide-ranging memory-search devices, internal controls over data that were not possible in the past. However, manual systems of accounting, although they involve great quantities of slow-moving paper, offer a certain security in that the paper goes through many different clerical and supervisory hands, which means that a successful fraud has to pass the repeated scrutiny of a number of people. But with computerized systems, in which literally tons of paperwork may be compressed into recorded signals on a single reel of magnetic tape, the number of people in the chain is vastly reduced. This tends to put far more information than before into the hands of far fewer people than before, and the capacity for abuse thus tends to be increased. Furthermore, the manual system requires clerks to sign vouchers, whereas computers impose anonymity. "When I type a computer entry into the record from a keyboard terminal, it looks just the same as if you had typed it," one computer-security man with considerable experience in banking systems remarked to me in discussing the vulnerabilities of computer systems. "In a multi-terminal computer system, there is simply no way of telling with certainty who is pushing the keys at the other end." Also, because of the extreme complexity of any computer system, it is difficult to check on just what a computer programmer, designer of a particular program, computer-tape librarian, or computer user may have been doing. Certainly, such matters tend to be almost entirely opaque to top management people in many organizations, and they are difficult even for auditors to comprehend fully. As Brandt Allen, a computer scientist at the Colgate Darden Graduate School of Business Administration of the University of Virginia, wrote in 1975 in a *Harvard Business Review* article on computer crime, "Computer technology tends to confound auditors and managers to the extent that they are rarely in a position to detect or prevent computer-based embezzlement."

Indeed, the number of successful computer frauds that have been committed against companies whose books have been found in order by reputable auditing firms has raised some serious questions in the financial press and in government about whether the auditing profession today is adequately protecting the public interest. These questions were underlined when, in September 1976, after a three-year investigation into the many-dimensioned Equity Funding fraud, the Securities and Exchange Commission accused the well-known accounting firm of Seidman & Seidman of negligence when it audited the Equity Funding books and declared them to be acceptable accounts of the company's true financial position. (The firm was also accused of negligence when it audited the books of three other companies in trouble with the S.E.C.) The S.E.C. made clear its belief that although the actual deceptions—primarily the practice of listing fictional dead souls as holders of live insurance policies—had been carried out by Seidman & Seidman's client, the conduct of the accounting firm itself "represented a breach of its ethical and professional responsibilities." The Commission maintained that, contrary to the representations of the accounting firm, the audits of Equity Funding were not carried out in accordance with generally accepted accounting procedures, that critical areas of the audits had been undertaken by inadequately trained people, and that the firm had placed "unwarranted reliance on management representations." The S.E.C. issued a formal administrative order instructing Seidman & Seidman to improve its auditing procedures.

A vice-president handling computer security in one large New York bank has little faith in the idea that the auditing profession can improve its ability to detect computer crimes in the making. "Auditors seldom find a loss," he told me. "They may confirm it after it happens." Other computer-security people are even more skeptical on this score. "The beautiful part about a computer crime is that if you're intent on committing one you can always make Column A equal Column B for the accountants," the independent computer-security consultant, Lindsay L. Baird, Jr., remarked. Donn Parker has observed that one basic problem affecting the auditor's detection of irregularities in computerized accounts is that in dealing with digitized material the auditor is at least once removed from the contents of the original record; he is essentially examining data representing the work of computer-terminal operators, computer programmers, magnetic-tape librarians, and electronics engineers. "Dealing with a computerized system tends to destroy the independence of the auditor, since the very people whose work he is supposed to be auditing are standing between him and the documents of record transmitted by these people," Parker told me.

In computer systems, what accountants call "the audit trail," by which auditors are supposedly able to trace transactions backward and forward, is at times inadequately marked. In manual systems, the audit trail consists of journals, ledgers, and other documents, all present before the auditor's eyes. But in a computerized accounting system, as Foster Brown, a computer-systems-development expert, wrote in an article in the *Journal of Systems Management* in April 1975, "the form, content, and accessibility of records frequently are such that the auditor is unable to follow a single transaction completely through the system." The impediments, Brown wrote, include the problem that source documents, once put into computer-readable form, tend to become relatively inaccessible, and in some computer systems are even eliminated. Brown also noted that "ledger summaries may be replaced by master files that do not show the amounts leading up to the summarized values." Above all, Brown said, the ability of the auditor to take a direct look at the figures involved is hindered by the fact that "files maintained on a magnetic medium cannot be read except by use of the computer and a computer program"—and, as Parker, too, pointed out, the computer and its program are generally run not by the auditor but by the people being audited. He has said, "The system is sufficiently complex so that if an auditor of the computerized books of a large corporation were to be truly independent in his examination, he would have to bring with him for the auditing process not only his own team of computer specialists but even his own computer."

In the course of my researches, I called on Donald L. Adams, managing director of administrative services for the American Institute of Certified Public Accountants, a trade association, about half of whose members are auditors, and asked him to explain his group's position on the problems of auditing computerized company books that might have been tainted by fraud. Adams said that as far as the auditing profession is concerned, "basically, our goal is to come up with a representation of the fairness of the financial statement set forth." He went on, "As a result, we have disclaimed that it is our responsibility to detect fraud. Certainly, many of the things we do in an audit might uncover fraud, and if we do we bring it to the attention of the client." A "Statement on Auditing Standards," issued by the American Institute of Certified

Public Accountants, limits the responsibility of the auditor in even more determined language. It states, in part, "The auditor recognizes that fraud, if sufficiently material, may affect his opinion on the financial statements." It goes on, "However, the ordinary examination . . . is not primarily or specifically designed, and cannot be relied upon, to disclose defalcations and other similar irregularities, although their discovery may result." And it insists that the responsibility of the auditor to detect fraud "arises only when such failure [to detect fraud] clearly results from failure to comply with generally accepted auditing standards." Adams said in his talk with me that, with certain exceptions, the financial impact of computer-related fraud is not great. "The sort of frauds that have taken place, while the amounts involved might seem high, have not been what in our parlance we term material; that is, they have not had a major impact on the fairness of a financial statement," he said. This, he made clear, was the official position of the auditors' association. Speaking unofficially, he conceded that it might be difficult to sustain that position in all cases of computer fraud, and certainly in the case of the Equity Funding affair. He asserted that most large accounting firms had people on their staffs who specialized in the auditing of computer systems and who were highly qualified to audit data from computers.

The handling of more and more computerized information—or digitized money, so to speak—by fewer and fewer people and the increase in the inherent risks involved have accelerated a trend toward eliminating the few human beings left in the computer-communication chain. This trend is apparent both in the area of electronic fund transfers, notably between banking institutions, and in government accounting systems, in which many billing and payment functions are carried out almost entirely by computer. One of the largest banks in New York is estimated to engage in computerized fund transfers of about $30 billion a day. A significant part of this traffic has now been completely automated. "We will guarantee to some of our customers that the transactions in which they are involved will not be touched by human hands," a vice-president of this bank told me. He added, "The reason the customers like the service is that computers don't make errors; people do."

However, a report issued in 1976 by the General Accounting Office, an investigative arm of Congress, on the automated decision-making by computers in government was not sanguine about heavy reliance on the untouched-by-human-hands approach—at least, on the federal level. According to the report, government computers each year issue, on an automated and unreviewed basis, authorizations for payments or checks (not including payroll checks) totaling $26 billion; the computers also issue unreviewed bills totaling $10 billion and unreviewed requisition orders, shipping orders, repair schedules, and the like valued at $8 billion. Altogether, according to the G.A.O. report, federal computers are involved in more than 1.5 billion separate payments and other actions a year "without anybody reviewing or evaluating whether they are correct." The G.A.O. found that designers, programmers, and users of electronic data-processing equipment made numerous errors, which were the cause of millions of dollars of wasted expenditure; it also found that the data being processed were not subject to adequate internal audits. Concerning the latter aspect, the G.A.O. report observed, "We learned that certain internal-audit groups rarely became involved in the [computer] applications' logic because they lacked the expertise to effectively make such studies."

In a separate report, the G.A.O. noted that "the number of computer-related crimes in government as well as in the private sector is cause for concern about how well systems are being controlled." (Excerpts from the report appear in Appendix 2.) This report said that the G.A.O. had learned of sixty-nine computer-related crimes or other incidents occurring within the government, and that these crimes had resulted in losses of more than $2 million, but it emphasized that the sixty-nine episodes were only those that had come to light, and stated that "we cannot be sure whether ... we simply have not uncovered larger crimes." Concerning the adequacy of internal controls within government agencies, the G.A.O. report said that "federal agencies' internal audit groups vary greatly" in how they review the integrity of computer-processing systems, and that in nine of twelve cases studied "auditors had not reviewed controls in the systems involved." Further, it observed, "Agency internal auditors often had not been informed about computer-related crimes so they could consider their effect on audit procedures. In several of the cases we reviewed, auditors told us our inquiry was the first time they had heard of the crimes."

In yet another report, in July 1977, on the computer-security program governing the processing of the confidential tax data on millions of U.S. taxpayers by the

Internal Revenue Service, the G.A.O. pointed out that while the I.R.S. computer system could "with proper design and implementation" provide a high level of protection for the confidentiality of taxpayers' records, the existing system contains weaknesses. Indeed, the G.A.O. declared, under present circumstances, "I.R.S.' [computer] security program [for processing tax information] does not assure confidentiality. Its security safeguards could easily be penetrated—especially by I.R.S. employees and others having access to the facilities. Such individuals could obtain access to tax returns or income tax data on a large, random number of taxpayers with little chance of detection. Employees, depending on the position occupied, could make unauthorized access to tax data on preselected taxpayers."

The G.A.O. said that while the known unlawful disclosures of computerized I.R.S. tax data have been few, "the relatively small number of known unauthorized disclosures was not due to a lack of opportunity." It further declared:

Inadequate controls over computer operations afforded many opportunities for I.R.S. employees and others to disclose tax data unlawfully. Computer programmers could easily run an unauthorized program or make an unauthorized program change without detection. Magnetic tapes, each containing tax data on as many as 5,000 taxpayers, were not properly controlled and some could not be accounted for. Computer printed products also were not controlled so that I.R.S. could be sure that they were received only by authorized persons.

Controls were exercised inadequately over I.R.S.' primary computerized data retrieval system. The system includes 4,000 terminals which enable about 18,600 authorized users to have instantaneous access to many taxpayer accounts. Many users can access data on any taxpayer except those few whose accounts I.R.S. has restricted. Service center users had use of system codes allowing access to data they did not need. Tapes containing system security information and manuals describing the built-in system security features were not secured adequately.

Employees were able to get unneeded tax data because I.R.S. was not enforcing its policy of limiting employee access to only that data needed to perform official duties. For example:

—Some I.R.S. installations permitted almost wholesale entry to restricted areas containing sensitive tax data.

—Some I.R.S. supervisors were not reviewing tax data requests or spot checking the data obtained to determine whether the requester officially needed it.

One of the I.R.S. computer systems is its data-retrieval system. It contains, on a selective basis, computerized records on about 10 percent of all U.S. taxpayers. The system can be accessed through about 4,000 visual display terminals, through which about 18,000 authorized service-center, district-office, and local-office users can take these actions:

They can instantaneously access a taxpayer's account.
They can view the recorded data on a visual display screen, and also cause a paper printout to be made of the same data.
They can change the recorded data.
They can cause taxpayer notices of various kinds to be mailed.
They can request original tax returns or photocopies.
They can have records for almost any taxpayer placed on the system.

Could I.R.S. employees with access to this system make changes beneficial to them in their own tax accounts lodged in this system? According to the G.A.O., "The [I.R.S.] security manual states that accessing or changing one's own tax account is a security violation which will be reported on the daily [I.R.S. computer] security report." In a test of the efficiency of this security system in July 1975, G.A.O. representatives set out to determine how readily an unauthorized person could penetrate the security screen of "command codes" governing valid entries into the system from its thousands of terminals. As a result, not only did the G.A.O. people manage successfully to change both their employee and terminal identification codes, but they also altered "security command codes" assigned to security supervisors. Indeed, they reported, "in our July 1975 testing we succeeded in issuing ourselves a refund by using a combination of command codes."

Lindsay Baird has given me one interesting example of computer crime involving the misuse of I.R.S. computers and the doctoring of data fed into and issued from them. "The incident happened a few years ago in a town in southern California," Baird said. "A woman had gone to a bank there to cash an Internal Revenue Service tax-refund check made out to her. She had all the proper personal identification with her, but a bank employee happened to recall from other checks the woman had cashed there that she was on public assistance, and felt puzzled by the federal-tax refund. She told her superior at the bank, the I.R.S. was notified, and the I.R.S. looked into the matter. They found that they had no record of having sent such a check to the woman. An

investigation—in which I had a part—followed. It turned
out that the woman had a niece working in California for
the I.R.S. as a data-terminal operator. One day, the niece
asked her aunt if she would like to have some government money. The woman said she would. So her relative
at the I.R.S. got the woman's Social Security number
from her, and with that she created in the I.R.S. computer system a fictitious tax record for her. The niece
knew the sequence of the I.R.S. computing process. The
I.R.S. uses ten regional computers around the country,
and maintains a master computer in West Virginia.
Hung on the ten regional computers, of course, are terminals. Through one of these terminals, the operator instructed the regional computer that the woman was owed
a tax refund for a certain amount. She knew just what
she was doing. The instruction was registered in the regional computer and passed on from that computer into
the master computer in West Virginia. The master computer wrote the woman a refund check at the appropriate
time in the programmed check-writing cycle. Then, after
the check-writing cycle had been completed, the operator
deleted the record from the regional computer, which
then updated the master computer on the change,
whereupon the master computer deleted the fictitious record that had been compiled, and also deleted the record
of its ever having written the woman a refund check. In
this case, the guilty operator was identified in the investigation. But the question remained as to whether this
was the only such case of altering I.R.S. records and
affecting its check-writing functions. The I.R.S. people had
no practical way of finding out how many operators might
have been doing the same sort of thing. The cost of audit-

ing and investigating so many people—so many relatives and friends of terminal operators—was so monumental that the I.R.S. people just gave up. They wanted to find a way of patching up the system to prevent similar incidents, of course, but I told them that it couldn't be done—that, among other things, the system had not been designed with auditability in mind."

As the result of such revelations of security weaknesses in I.R.S. computer systems—and, in particular, the critical 1977 G.A.O. report—the Commissioner of the I.R.S., while conceding that the I.R.S. had not been as aggressive in the past as it might have been in correcting situations that potentially weakened its overall security, declared that he is committing the Internal Revenue Service to a "vigorous course of improvement" in the management of computerized tax data in order to assure maximum security for information on taxpayers.

The difficulties of catching up with the people who have committed computer crimes is compounded by the reluctance of corporations to talk about the fact that they have been defrauded and by the difficulties and embarrassments of prosecution and trial. In instance after instance, corporations whose assets have been plundered—whose computer operations have been left shattered by wiped-out memory functions or have been manipulated to churn out fictitious accounting data or to print large checks to the holders of dummy accounts—have preferred to suffer in silence rather than to have the horrid facts about the frailty of their miracle processing systems come to public attention.

Top management people in large corporations fear that

publicity about internal fraud could well affect their companies' trading position on the stock market, hold the corporations up to public ridicule, and cause all sorts of turmoil within their staffs. In many cases, it seems, management will go to great lengths to keep the fact of an internal computer crime from its own stockholders. People who commit computer crimes tend to be aware of management's extreme sensitivity to publicity on the subject, and when their defalcations happen to be discovered they sometimes take advantage of that sensitivity to bargain their way out of serious trouble.

One example of the unabashed use of management fear of publicity arising out of such abuses has been cited by Gerald McKnight, a British writer who is the author of a book called *Computer Crime*. According to McKnight, a young manager of the sales department of a company in the English Midlands voted with other directors of his company to computerize its accounting operations. He thereafter began systematically looting the company treasury through its computer by establishing dummy companies, to whose accounts he instructed the computer to write a steady stream of checks. His crime was eventually uncovered partly through the resentment of a computer keypunch clerk, whom he had burdened with unpaid overtime work that happened to consist of entering his fraudulent instructions into the company's accounting system. Upon being confronted with the fraud, the criminal calmly admitted his misdeeds, but his fellow-directors pointed out to the chairman of the board that any prosecution would result in publicity that could have serious effects on the company's reputation for efficient control of its affairs. The former sales manager went on to demand coolly that the company give him a letter of recommendation so that he could find satisfactory work elsewhere. Rather than face unpleasant publicity, his employers caved in and gave him the recommendation, whereupon the computer criminal moved to another company as its executive director and, for three and a half years thereafter, steadily manipulated *its* computer to pay money out into dummy accounts, at the rate of about $100,000 a year. After a long internal investigation into inconsistencies that were eventually discovered in the company's accounts, the crime was brought to light. And once again the criminal admitted his guilt, and managed to walk away with a letter of recommendation to his next prospective employer. But the malefactor's boldness tripped him up. Before leaving the second company, he had the effrontery to demand that the second company pay him a lump sum of about $6,000 to cover "loss of office"—a separation payment to which, under British law, executives are entitled under certain circumstances. At that, the indignation of the directors of the second company simply could not be contained; not only did they refuse to pay but they took legal action against him, though not on criminal charges. They started a civil suit against him, charging breach of contract.

The reluctance of corporations to subject themselves to unfavorable publicity over computer crimes is so great that some corporations actually seem willing to take the risk of getting into trouble with the law themselves by concealing crimes committed against them. Among independent computer-security consultants, it is widely suspected that certain banks, which seem exceptionally reluctant to admit that such a thing as computer fraud even exists in the banking fraternity, do not always report such crimes to the Comptroller of the Currency, in Washington, when they occur, as all banks are required to do by federal law. Bank officers do not discuss the details of computer crimes with the press. Neither do officials at the office of the Comptroller of the Currency, who claim that existing statutes forbid them to do so. Thus the banks seem effectively protected from detailed public examination of the degree to which they really do comply with the law. "The bank doesn't want to look as if its security were bad," one independent computer-security man said to me in explaining the reluctance of some banks to comply with that law. Donn Parker, who believes he has almost certain knowledge of at least one major bank computer crime that was never reported to the federal government, told me that a principal reason for this kind of behavior is the fear on the part of banks that such a record will bring about an increase in their insurance rates; and he explained that the terms of their contracts for insurance against robbery or other crimes are among the most confidential and jealously guarded information in the banks' possession.

In addition to the problems of detecting and bringing computer crimes to light, there are the difficulties of effectively prosecuting computer criminals. In the first place, the police, if they are to collect evidence, have to be able to understand precisely how a crime may have been committed, and that usually calls for the kind of technical knowledge that is simply not available to most police departments. Even on a federal rather than a local law-enforcement level, few members of prosecutorial staffs know enough about the intricacies of electronic data processing to prepare a case against defendants which will stand up in court. The Federal Bureau of Investigation has developed a course in computer criminology at its agent-training center, at Quantico, Virginia, but, according to commercial computer-security people I have talked with, the training so far offered is not of a very advanced type in relation to all the ramifications of the existing criminal problems. Another difficulty is that not only police and prosecutors but juries and judges must be able to find their way through the mass of technical detail before they can render verdicts and hand down decisions in cases of computer crime, and this alone is a demanding task. In the face of all the complexities involved and all the time necessary to prepare a case that will stand up in court, many prosecutors try to make the best accommodation they can with the defendants' lawyers by plea bargaining, or else they simply allow the cases to fade away unprosecuted. If they do bring a case to trial, they have the problem of presenting evidence that is acceptable to the court.

August Bequai, who is a former member of the enforcement staff of the S.E.C., and who, besides being a practicing lawyer in Washington, was once the chairman of a Federal Bar Association subcommittee on white-collar crime, says that the big stumbling block for prosecutors in computer-crime cases is the introduction of digitized information as acceptable evidence. "Suppose you bring a case involving a crime committed through manipulation of a computer, and you try to introduce a computer printout as evidence of the crime," Bequai explains.

"You immediately run into what is called the hearsay rule, which says that at a trial you can't introduce into the court record a statement made outside the courtroom unless it represents a record of an act, transaction, occurrence, or event made contemporaneously with the act at issue, and in the ordinary course of business. Such an acceptable record would be the notation made by a nurse in a doctor's office as to what time a patient came in to see the doctor on a particular day. But when it comes to introducing computer printouts as a record to support a prosecution case, the prosecution has to reckon with the fact that they haven't necessarily been made in the regular course of business or made contemporaneously with the acts at issue—they may have been run off some time after the actual crime. In matters of fraud, you have to prove who falsified what records and when, and produce evidence to that effect, but it's extremely difficult to produce evidence of precisely what happened throughout the whole computing process, with all its stages—the input at entry terminals, the programming of the data, the storage and all the processing that take place in the computer room itself, the production by the computer of punch-card decks representing the processed data, and, of course, the eventual printouts, which might be made in remote spots thousands of miles away. And then you have to contend with how material these electronic signals are considered to be under the law. Suppose someone steals—physically makes off with—paper securities. That's a clear case of theft, of something whose face value is clearly printed on the stolen securities. But what if a thief steals a reel of computer tape bearing the same information as the paper securities but in digitized form?

Under many state laws, the prosecution may have a hard time proving in court that the thief has stolen money. What he has made off with may be downgraded to a reel of magnetic tape so what is actually grand larceny becomes a case of petit larceny."

The status of electronic data impulses as property is as yet so undefined and unclear in many criminal statutes that the findings of a California judge in the case of Eli Bart—which, as the reader will recall, involved the theft of a valuable program from the computer of another company—is likely to be a precedent in computer-crime jurisprudence. In considering how Bart used his employer's computer keyboard terminal and printout system to extract, via telephone line, the program in question from a competing company's computer, the judge found that, under a California law protecting trade secrets, electronic data impulses that Bart had caused to be transmitted from the competitor's computer did not constitute an "article," or a tangible form, representing a trade secret. What the court did find was that the material in question was essentially "a private library," to which Bart had obtained access without a proper library card, consisting of the secret passwords and so on that were necessary for authorized users. The act of theft, the court found, was not in Bart's stealing electronic impulses over the telephone line but only in his stealing their tangible form; in other words, the theft consisted of Bart's having caused his employer's computer to make a printout of the pirated program and his physically carrying the printout from his employer's computer into his nearby office.

In essence, then, the court's finding was that although

the electronic impulses that Bart had extracted from the competing company's computer did not have the standing of a trade secret, the paper printout of those same impulses constituted a *copy* of a trade secret, and the copying activity involved was actionable under California law. By this rather tortuous reasoning by the court, it appears that if Bart had dispensed with the printout and had fed the purloined data directly into his own computer, or displayed it on a visual screen instead of causing it to be printed out on paper, he would, under California law, have committed no crime.

A most interesting summary of the problems associated with detecting, collecting evidence on, and successfully prosecuting computer crimes is contained in a statement submitted to the U.S. Senate Committee on Government Operations, in November 1976, during the course of a committee staff study of computer security in federal programs, by Richard Thornburgh, then Assistant Attorney General for the Criminal Division of the Department of Justice. The statement is worth quoting from at some length.

Thornburgh began by declaring that investigations carried out by the General Accounting Office "confirm what many have suspected—that computers may well be out of control." Even as a layman who had no specific training in the machinations of the computer, Thornburgh said, he was not surprised by the revelations by the G.A.O. concerning computer crime in government. He added, "If it takes a publisher's computer months to acknowledge the change of address on my magazine subscription, I can imagine how long it will take an inventory control computer to acknowledge the disappearance of merchandise from some far-flung regional warehouse. If we are billed for merchandise we never bought, it is not unreasonable to conclude that someone may be buying merchandise for which they are never billed." And he asked, "If in its first twenty-seven months of operation, the Social Security Administration's new federal welfare computer will have permitted some $620 million in apparently negligent overpayments—as a recent H.E.W. audit revealed—have we not created an irresistible temptation for fraud?"

The Assistant Attorney General then went on to discuss computer crime in terms of three broad categories: the computer as victim, the computer as an environment for crime, and the computer as accomplice. In the first of these categories, where the computer may be the physical target of the arsonist, the vandal, the extortionist, these are traditional crimes evoking a traditional response from law-enforcement bodies. But, he said, they nonetheless raise novel questions concerning the universal spread of computer-data processing—a central question being this: by continuing to concentrate information and decisionmaking in centralized data systems, are we overexposing our society to the threats of the extortionist or the intimidation of the vandal? Thornburgh estimated, for example, that 60 percent of the banks in this country could not open for business tomorrow if, tonight, the computers processing their demand deposits failed. And he pointed out that as we come to rely increasingly on the computer to perform the basic functions of society—as, for example, we move into the era of electronic fund transfers, computerized stock exchanges, and central data banks—the vulnerability of government, business, citizens, and customers inevitably increases. As for the second category, he said that the experience of the Department of Justice has been that the largest incidence of computer crime today falls under this general heading. But he said that the third category, in which the computer is made an accomplice of crime, is of increasing concern, especially in those cases where highly trained and highly skilled people manipulate the computer so that it becomes an integral part of their schemes to carry out the theft of computer time, programs, sensitive information, cash, and other assets. "These schemes range from the simple to the highly complex," Thornburgh said. "On one hand, a bank programmer may insert a single 'patch' in the bank computer program which will cause the system to ignore his overdrafts. Other more sophisticated 'computerniks' engage in complex cryptography to break the computer's access code, manipulate the internal systems in order to perpetrate the crime, and then program the computer to destroy all traces of the unauthorized intrusion." He declared that while there may be a great temptation on the part of some computer users and law-enforcement officials to dismiss this brand of computer crime as science fiction, "to do so would be a serious mistake," since "it is a reality today and in all probability will constitute the majority of computer crime in the future."

As an example, he discussed the supposed technical difficulty of obtaining or altering computer-stored data protected at its access terminals by a five-digit access code known only to authorized users. To break that code by a trial-and-error method would require 100,000 combinations, a routine that would deter the average person from such an approach. But for the intruder with a computer accomplice, these difficulties are of another order. Thornburgh said: "In one instance, the user of a time-sharing system with general access to the computer wanted to get access to information locked in a higher security level beyond his authorization; he programmed the victim's own computer to try all possible combinations of the higher level access code. Several seconds and several thousand combinations later, the computer successfully picked the lock."

He continued, "The prosecution of computer crime is hindered by a number of factors. Computer crime is a low-visibility proposition. There are no smoking pistols—no blood-stained victims; often the crime is detected by sheer accident. Recently, a squib buried in the business section of a Washington newspaper caught my attention. The gist of the article was that a major industrial firm had relocated its toy division. In the relocation process, it suspended its computer operation and conducted a physical inventory, only to discover $1.5 million in missing inventory. In all probability if it had not been for the fortuitous relocation, the deficit would have widened."

Then, compounding the difficulties, there is that problem of the reluctance of corporate computer users to report computer abuse because of the embarrassment that such disclosure might bring them. Thornburgh gave this example: "In a recent case brought to my attention, an outside audit commissioned by bank officials confirmed that a computer programmer had manipulated the bank's data system and embezzled $250,000. However, fundamental errors in the design and implementation of the bank's computer system had resulted in an additional $10 million in losses through negligent overpayments, miscalculated interest, and uncollected charges. The bank directors were in no mood for the publicity of a public prosecution. They took the position that the embezzler had done them a great service by exposing the deficiencies of their system and saving them from an avalanche of shareholder suits and possibly bankruptcy."

The Assistant Attorney General went on to discuss the curiously ambivalent attitude of computer users toward certain aspects of security: "Consider the businessman who would never leave his checkbook lying on top of his desk—who requires a double signature on each corporate check—who would never discharge a sensitive employee without changing the lock on the door and the combination of the office safe—and who would be aghast if his banker informed him that as an economy measure the bank was no longer returning canceled checks. This same businessman will purchase a multimillion dollar computer system from an energetic salesman without an audit as basic as a canceled check—will place a computer terminal on top of the desk unattended—will use one programmer to design his entire computer system—and will discharge his programmer without making the most rudimentary changes in his computer's security system."

He then discussed in detail the legal difficulties of prosecuting different varieties of computer crime under the numerous existing federal statutes relating to theft and embezzlement, and certain recently added definitions in the Federal Rules of Evidence that, he felt, would assist prosecutors in presenting acceptable evidence in such cases. Nonetheless, he said, the prosecution still has the burden of establishing the authenticity of computer records in computer-crime cases by introducing evidence describing the particular data-processing system involved in a case and demonstrating that the system produces an accurate result. This will require the most careful witness preparation to insure that prosecution experts can communicate in a language that the court can understand. And he observed that such authentication may be difficult for a computer system with a track record of malfunction or without those error-detection devices commonly used in the electronic data-processing industry.

Then, in other prosecutions based on common law concepts there are additional problems, Thornburgh pointed out. For example, the distinction between theft and grand theft is muddied where stolen property is information whose monetary value may be difficult for the court to determine. And in the large time-sharing data-processing systems which are the trend today, thousands of individual corporate and institutional users of computers commingle their data in central files with loose security restrictions and, in general, in such a manner that at an actual trial involving computer theft the concept of trade secrets and the even more basic distinction between public and private property may be lost on the jury trying the case.

Then again, there remains the problem of physically gathering adequate evidence for trial in computer crimes. Thus:

[It] may be increasingly important to seize the suspect's books and records before they can be altered or destroyed; the investigator may be forced to rely increasingly on the search warrant procedure. The prosecutor must have sufficient knowledge of the computer system to draft a warrant that is broad enough to reach the evidence but sufficiently narrow to withstand challenge. Nor would it be productive for the investigator to arrive on the scene with a valid search warrant if he cannot get the data out of the machine or to put a guard at the door if the computer operator inside can instantaneously destroy evidence with the push of a button. These new circumstances must be carefully understood and explained to the magistrate at the time a search warrant is requested. Extraordinary procedures may be warranted; the Government may be obliged to seek a court-appointed receiver to assume operation of the data system to insure the evidence is not destroyed and to enable the Government to recover data in a meaningful format.

Once the prosecutor has obtained his evidence, he must be aware of still other technological peculiarities. Information stored in a computer memory is extremely volatile. Magnetic tapes and discs must be stored at carefully controlled temperatures and atmospheric conditions. The prosecutor who locks a computer tape in a file cabinet of a Government building with no air-conditioning on the weekends, may inadvertently destroy his evidence or at least expose [its integrity] to challenge by the defendant's more computer-wise attorney.

Under present circumstances, even when people who carry out computer-related crimes do manage to be convicted under existing laws, they are seldom sent to prison, and even when they are, they usually receive sentences that are remarkably light compared with those imposed on people convicted of commoner forms of larceny. In part, this leniency can be explained by the generally nonviolent nature of the offenses, their sheer novelty to most judges, and, possibly, the impersonal nature of the victims chosen by the defendants. Furthermore, nearly all the defendants are members of the white-collar class, and so are generally deemed to be good risks for rehabilitation; compared with people accused of street larceny, say, most of the convicted people fare well in the presentencing reports prepared by probation departments, whose researchers tend to work within a structure of solid bourgeois values. For a computer embezzlement of $1.5 million from the Union Dime Savings Bank in New York, Hattner, the chief teller in the Park Avenue branch of the bank, received a sentence of twenty months in jail. (This sentence led one computer-security man to remark to me, "If a man takes money from a bank teller and doesn't even use a gun but only shoves a note at the teller, he'll get five years. [Hattner's] haul of a million and a half dollars is the equivalent of his having committed a bank-branch robbery once a day for three years at the rate of the typical branch holdup take, which is about two thousand dollars.")

For his use of the Pacific Telephone & Telegraph Company's computer to steal $1 million worth of equipment, Jerry Schneider was sentenced to sixty days in jail, and was freed after serving a bit more than a month. In the case of Eli Bart, the presentencing report noted, "Computer-program theft is the crime of the future. As such, it has not been referred to this [probation] office at the felony level in prior instances. Thus, there is no ready frame of reference for determining a proper sentence." Bart got three years' probation and a $5,000 fine. One ringleader of a gang that police charged had, in 1971, recruited insiders at two credit-reporting bureaus—TRW Credit Data and the Computer Credit Corporation—to establish false identities and credit records in the computers of these companies was, after pleading guilty to charges of making false financial statements, placed on probation and fined $1,000. The ringleader of another gang that was alleged to have penetrated TRW Credit Data, between 1973 and 1974, and inserted false credit data in its computers was also placed on probation and fined $1,000 on similar charges. A computer-terminal operator inside another credit-reporting bureau, called Equifax, Inc., who was alleged to have participated in a scheme to feed fake credit data into company computers was not even taken to court. According to an article in the *Wall Street Journal* dealing with this affair, "Equifax actually declined to prosecute its suspected insider," because "prosecution was so difficult," and because the company had fired the terminal operator suspected of having participated in the scheme and considered the operator's dismissal penalty enough.

For the purpose of closing some of the loopholes in existing law that make it so difficult for prosecutors to bring computer criminals to account in the courts, Senator Abraham Ribicoff, of Connecticut, introduced a bill in the Senate in June 1977 that would make virtually any unauthorized use of federal computers or computer-processing systems, or similar private equipment or systems used in interstate commerce, a federal offense. The bill is designed to cover improper manipulations within a broad range of activities occurring in computer processing: input activity, involving the translation of data into computerized form and its storage on punch cards, magnetic tapes, or other devices; programming activity, which provides a logical sequence of instructions that direct the computer in solving problems; processing activity, in which data are handled according to the directions of a program; and output activity, where the end results of the data processing are made available to the computer user in printout or other form. The Ribicoff bill is also aimed at improper manipulations of computers or their data from remote locations, via telephone line, such as occurred in the Bart case. (For a more detailed summary of the proposed provisions of the Ribicoff bill, and of the conditions it is designed to remedy, see Appendix 1.)

6

Harlowe

There are certain exceptions to the history of lenient treatment of computer criminals who have been convicted. One such example is the case of a man I shall refer to as James Harlowe. In a northern California court, Harlowe was convicted of embezzling more than $1 million from his employer, a large produce-growing and packing company, by manipulating the computer that processed the company's accounts. Harlowe had carried out the embezzlement during a period of six years from a position of trust as the company's chief accountant. In essence, what Harlowe did was to use the computer to play a kind of digitized war game, in which he designated a master program that, when it was integrated into the company's computerized accounting system, would systematically siphon off large sums into dummy accounts and thus into his own pockets—all this in such a way that his crime would be virtually untraceable. And the scheme worked, year after year, without his employer's being any the wiser. It worked so well, in fact, that in the end, when Harlowe decided, for his own reasons, to have it known that an embezzlement had been going on, he encountered difficulty in drawing attention to the fact that his company's computerized books had been thoroughly cooked for a long period. When he was finally apprehended and found guilty of grand theft, he could easily have escaped with a light sentence, but before his sentencing he tactlessly displayed such a lack of remorse that the court was angered and he was given a ten-year term in prison. Of that term, he served five and a half years, in San Quentin. He is now in business for himself in northern California.

In the course of my travels in preparing this work, and while I was in California, I met Harlowe and had a long talk with him about his adventures as a computer criminal. I was not able to discuss his case with his former employers, because I had already learned on good authority that they, like the officers of most other corporations that have been victims of computer crime, had no intention of talking with the press. And, of course, what I got from Harlowe is his side of the events in which he became enmeshed.

My initial meeting with Harlowe was over a leisurely lunch in a restaurant. He is a rather short, sandy-haired man in his mid-forties, with brown eyes and horn-rimmed glasses. His manner was brisk and attentive. In arranging the interview, I had assured him that I would not use his real name in writing about his case, and he answered my questions—even those I felt a bit awkward about phrasing, such as "Just when did you begin your embezzlement?"—with a cheerful responsiveness.

Harlowe comes from a ranch-owning family whose

roots were established in northern California over several generations; he appears sufficiently proud of the social solidity of his family background to bear himself with a faintly patrician air. In college, in California, he majored in economics and statistical theory. After he graduated from college, in the early 1950s, he worked for a while as a civil engineer. He spent the summer of 1961 on a leave of absence in an area south of San Francisco, where a friend told him that a large produce company nearby was having administrative and accounting problems, because a couple of employees on whom the company depended had left. On the friend's recommendation, Harlowe went to see the president of the produce company, and he was hired as an administrator and accountant. Harlowe ran the company's packing-shed operations, in which 150 people were employed, and took on the responsibility of supervising all the accounting for the company's operations. He told me that the work was demanding but that he was well paid, and that at the end of his first seven-month growing cycle the president of the company gave him a $10,000 bonus in appreciation of the order he had brought into the company's operations. However, Harlowe said, he found his employers difficult to deal with; he felt they were "coarse," "insensitive," and "bullying" in their relations with their employees. "They simply lacked gentility," he told me. He decided to leave, in spite of the pay, and with his bonus he bought an interest in a small chemical company. But the following year, he said, the people running the produce company asked him to come back to work, this time on a profit-sharing basis. "The company was grossing about thirty million dollars a year, and I was told that if I would come back they'd give me five percent of the pretax profit, plus a salary of twenty-five thousand dollars, plus expenses, plus a car and food for my family," Harlowe said. (He is married and has a large family.) He went on, "This was in 1962, and I felt I couldn't refuse the offer. So I went to work for them on that basis—as their chief administrator and accountant."

One innovation that Harlowe induced his employers to adopt was a fully computerized accounting system. For a couple of years before this, Harlowe told me, he had been studying computer technology and had been taking I.B.M. training courses in the subject; he had also developed his own library on electronic data processing. "After a while, I'd rented an I.B.M. 402 accounting machine and some ancillary equipment, such as card-punch equipment," he said. "I kept all this stuff in my garage—the way, I guess, someone else might put in an electric-train layout. I was really involved in computing and data processing." After Harlowe had been back at work with the company for a short time, he began to develop a way of automating the company's accounting system, using the equipment in his garage. "I wrote all the procedures and wired up the panels in the equipment," he said. "When I had the system well worked out, I set up an independent computer-service bureau, moved the data-processing equipment out of the garage, and set up in business—but not in my own name. I hired a few people and managed to get some data-processing work from various clients. This was quite aside from my regular job. In a while, I went to the management of the company and, without telling them what I had done, I persuaded them to automate their accounting system and to have the work done by a computer-service bureau. I recommended that they use the bureau I had set up." At that stage, he said, he had no thought of engaging in anything really wrong; his only reason for concealing his ownership of the service bureau was that he knew, as an accountant, that the auditors would expect the data processing of the company's accounts to be handled by a third and entirely independent party, but he really wanted to get the company's business, which was substantial. He got it, and his sideline computer-service business thrived. "I rented time on an I.B.M. 1401 computer, then got my own I.B.M. 360 on lease at three thousand dollars a month," Harlowe said. He also carried on his official accounting and administrative duties with the produce company.

At the end of the 1962 growing season, Harlowe said, he was in for a shock. The management appeared to be as pleased as ever with his services, but he found that instead of getting the expected 5 percent of the company's pretax profit as a bonus he got a greatly reduced figure. Before his 5-percent share was computed, the rest of the top management people took their shares from the pretax profit, and his share was figured on what remained of the pretax profit after the bonuses of the top management people had been subtracted. "I felt cheated," Harlowe told me. "I was angry. I hadn't had any liking for the people who were running the company in the first place. And I said to myself, 'There's one guy in this organization you shouldn't fool around with.' I was handling the money."

Harlowe decided that he would find his own way of getting back the percentage of the company's profit he believed himself to have been cheated out of. So in processing the company's accounts he ran them through the computer again, subjecting the data to alterations that gave the accounts the appearance of being conscientiously compiled and properly balanced, but, at the same time, diverting funds to himself. The diverted funds were accounted for in the computerized books mostly in the form of various increased costs. Harlowe then began to loot the corporation's gross at what he considered the acceptable rate of three-quarters of one percent annually. He did this by devising a special algorithm—a set of rules for making calculations—which he used as a master program to alter the company's accounting data in the computer. "The algorithm allowed me to assess true cost variances in the accounts and to inflate these in a way that seemed reasonable," he said. "When you're doing millions of dollars' worth of business it isn't all that difficult to make alterations in increments of pennies or fractions of cents. I would subject the company records to these variances in the computer in such a way as to diffuse the higher costs throughout the system."

Harlowe kept the true computer records of the company's financial position; the company got the altered version in printout form. "What made the elevated cost figures relatively easy to justify was the nature of the produce business, which is subject to many fluctuations," he said. "For example, you have continuous fluctuations in such matters as freight and labor costs. And you have weather. If we had a period of rainy weather, I would build in a little extra to the naturally increased harvesting costs resulting from this, and could always easily justify these increases. After all, who can tell exactly how muddy a muddy condition is? I'd pick other natural phenomena to which, at what seemed the right time, I could attribute some other elevated cost factor. As the chief accountant, I made a weekly report to the managers of the company on the state of their accounts, and I'd take with me a printout of the altered records. I might tell them at one meeting that the cost of carrots was running at, say, twenty-eight dollars a ton. I might have escalated the cost, through the computer processing, by a factor of seventy-five cents a ton, but the algorithm controlling the accounting data had so spread the added cost through the system that it was integrated into a huge variety of very detailed information—so much for row-boss supervision, so much for harvest labor, so much for trucking, so much for tractor overhead, so much for fertilizer and pesticides. The increased cost shown penetrated into almost every area of the company's operations. Once a week, I reviewed the extra costs that I felt I could safely build into the system. I took the company's true costs, decided on the variances, and, using the algorithm I'd devised, had the computer spread the costs in such a way as to support the total cost figure I had decided on. I had no elaborate figuring to do. It was all in the design. The whole arrangement was built into the computer system. It would be hard for anyone to believe that the cost figures shown in the finished printout could be wrong when they were supported by such a mass of information, in which all the details seemed to relate perfectly to one another. But, believe it or not, I didn't have to do much more than press a few buttons to achieve the effect. The algorithm was the key to the whole thing.

"In the kind of work I do, I happen to visualize cost-accounting problems in geometrical or spatial metaphors. I tend to see figures in the shape of charts and graphs; I tend to see a cost progression as a curve with a certain shape and in a certain motion across a scale. When you see things that way, you don't need to burden yourself with a million details. Once I had visualized how I wanted the cost curve to go in relation to the real costs of the operation, I made the cost adjustments I thought appropriate—two cents a box of produce now, a cent later on—and the computer went through all the details and expanded all the cost minutiae to fit the new cost configuration. I really had what you might call an econometric model of the company's operations, including the whole banking array. As a matter of fact, some of the ideas for the model were based on principles I'd learned while I was a student in college. My professor in statistics then was Kenneth Arrow, who is now at Harvard. He won the Nobel Prize a few years ago. I don't suppose it ever occurred to him that he might be training an embezzler. Well, the computer would tell me how much to spend in each cost category. To receive the difference between the real and the inflated costs, I had opened dummy bank accounts in the names of fictitious corporations that were presumably doing business with the produce company, operating from box numbers—a procedure that is very common in the produce business. All told, there were about fourteen dummy bank accounts having supposed dealings with the produce company. The difference between the inflated and the real costs would be funneled into these dummy accounts. Suppose I decided at the end of a particular month to create eight thousand dollars of inflated costs. The computer would break this down into cost categories, such as labor costs. I'd have a dummy company that would be a labor contractor, which I'd give a likely sounding name to. I would have a produce-company check of three thousand and sixty-two dollars made out to this company. The same thing with inflated packaging materials. The computer would move the surplus funds into these dummy accounts by check.

"Not all these dummy companies would receive money all the time, because I wanted to use some of them only at certain times. However, in order to keep up the appearance of activity in these dummy corporations I would have the computer write what was really a series of kited checks between these accounts and between these accounts and the company. It was a sort of perpetual-motion system—a movement of paper for appearance's sake—and to maintain it I would keep about twenty thousand dollars of supposed working capital shifting between the dummy accounts, so that there was always something in the pipeline. The algorithm took care of where to send the money, just as it did in the case of all the money I regularly siphoned off from the company treasury into the dummy accounts. The computer even wrote out the checks to the dummy companies. I just had to drop the checks off in the mail, along with the bank-deposit slips."

Harlowe said that he gradually stepped up the embezzlement until it was providing him—on top of his regular salary of $25,000 and his annual bonus of about $15,000—with $200,000 a year. During the six-year period of his embezzling, his average annual take was a little over $166,000. He said that although his employers

often complained about high operating costs, his accounting appeared to be entirely above suspicion. He told me
that sometimes, after inflating the costs of particular
types of produce, he would take his fraudulent weekly
computer printouts to the management and do some
complaining himself. "I'd go into these meetings with my
reports and say, 'Look at these costs—you've got to bring
down these unit costs in these areas.'" He went on, "And
after calling attention to the very conditions I was
changing I'd give them a convincing explanation of why
the costs were high. Then we'd develop a management
plan for correcting these high costs, and the next week
I'd let the conditions be corrected. But the week after that
the cost of something *else* would go up on the books."

"Innumerable as the sands of the sea are the passions
of man," wrote Nikolai Gogol in *Dead Souls,* musing on
the life of Tchitchikov, the book's restless hero, "and all
are different, and all, base and noble alike, are first
under a man's control, and afterward cruel tyrants
dominating him." The phantom labor-contracting
companies and their electronic dead souls who were
registered within the recesses of Harlowe's I.B.M.
360 exerted at times a direct influence on the fortunes
of the live souls who actually toiled in the produce
company's fields as pickers. Most of the thousand-odd
laborers in the company fields were Mexican nationals
brought to this country under contract as migratory
workers through the so-called bracero program. Although such people might not have known much about
computers, they knew a great deal about the rigors of
field work, and there were times when they had to work

harder than ever to satisfy the kind of Stakhanovite norms established in Harlowe's computerized accounts. As Harlowe described it, the effects of the manipulated contents of his computer on the lives of field hands began to be felt not long after the company switched to computerized accounting, and at first the changes were made on behalf of the company itself. Harlowe recalled, "The braceros had all been on piecework in the fields, and then the U.S. Department of Labor came along and laid down regulations that required each bracero to be paid at a minimum guaranteed hourly rate regardless of his piecework earnings. Naturally, this wasn't to the liking of the produce company, because it meant that the basis of pay was cut loose from the established piecework-production criteria. The braceros didn't understand anything about this guaranteed-wage stuff. One of the functions of the row bosses was to pound away at the idea that they were still on piece rates.

"The company came to me with the problem. I proposed a remedy. They told me to go ahead. So what I did was to write a computer program that would simulate payroll records. I used this simulation to devise a way in which we could optimize the relationship between hours worked and production achieved, and so make it appear that the braceros were working fewer hours than they actually were, and were thus making more than the minimum hourly wage called for by the Department of Labor regulations. I worked out such a scheme on the computer. In this scheme, I staggered—in the computer records, anyway—the supposed departure times of the buses that carried workers into the fields and grouped the men in different buses, so that individual workers whom the computer had identified from payroll records as being the best producers would always make up a crew that accounted for the greatest number of hours of work, and that crew's bus, as I caused the records to show, would be sent off into the fields first. Then I'd put the lesser producers into buses with later departure times, thereby reducing the number of hours they worked, and when all the time sheets and production records were computerized and compiled into printouts of payroll records the resulting figures optimized the braceros' piecework earnings per hour and put them over the required federal minimum. In the first season, that program saved the company seventy-eight thousand dollars." Put another way, it evidently cost the braceros $78,000. "The braceros weren't aware of the details, of course," Harlowe said. "They weren't so unhappy. Anyway, they were used to what they call *la mordida*—the bite. It was part of their life."

When Harlowe turned against his employers and organized his embezzlement, the concentration of his energies on this project left him little time to attempt to solve the problems of migratory labor. But as the embezzlement moved along its course, Harlowe was able to use some of his insight into field-working conditions to further his scheme. In explaining how he would rationalize higher costs shown in the books, Harlowe told me, "I'd go into one of these management meetings with my accounts that reflected inflated figures on harvesting costs. If the real harvesting costs for carrots happened to be twenty-five dollars a ton, my figures would show them to be thirty dollars a ton. The row-boss cost figures should come to five dollars and sixty cents a ton, but they would show as five dollars and seventy-five cents a ton. When I presented these figures, management would ask, 'How come the costs are so high here?' And I'd tell them that the figures showed they must be paying the field crews for bags of carrots that weren't full. That's the sort of thing you watch out for on piecework, you see. If you figure that your one-unit piece pay is equivalent to a bag of carrots weighing fifty pounds, and you accept bags that have only forty-nine pounds of carrots in them, you're getting only ninety-eight percent of the product contracted for. And I'd say to management, 'You've got to have these guys fill their bags of carrots.' And management would go out and try to make corrections. They would harass the row bosses, who would harass their crews. The row bosses would tell management, 'We're doing our best.' But they accepted management's explanation. Management would tell them, 'We've got it down here in black and white.' And management itself believed it. The computer figured it out, and who could argue with the facts?"

As Harlowe prospered, he made investments in the cattle business, maintained several cars, and flew his own light airplane, in which he traveled throughout the northern California valley regions in the course of doing outside, legitimate data-processing business with ranchers and farmers for his computer-service company. He also had two homes, for one of which, on the northern California coast, he paid $90,000. He felt he was making the best of the circumstances he found himself in. He told me, "There was the satisfaction of having the last word where the produce company was concerned. There was a personality conflict between the principals and me, and

I'm an egotist and don't like to be treated in a manner in which I'm expected to have a subservient attitude. Then, there was the excitement—it all seemed like a daring thing to do." At the same time, he said, what was happening to him had an unreal character. "Sometimes I had to stop and think that I was really doing all this." But there was also a sense of power. "It was as though I were the one in control of the situation. There was a sort of solitary grandeur."

I asked Harlowe whether he had ever dreamed at night about his embezzlement. He said he hadn't. I asked him if he daydreamed about the future. He said he had done a lot of that. He would imagine himself living a life of financial independence. "I wanted to be respected in my field," he told me. "I could see myself on the California coast in a new house I had built in my mind. It would have a nice library, and I would be getting visits from prominent people—the Under-Secretary of Labor, for example—and we would spend half the night arguing about agricultural policy; or a professor of mathematics I happened to respect, and we would sit in the library and discuss econometric models at length." Also, Harlowe thought about how he would greatly expand his legitimate computer-service business, and he saw himself as gaining recognition for computer-programming innovations he felt he could devise.

Harlowe's daydreaming did not prevent him from keeping his eyes open to what was going on around him. At the office where he maintained his commercial data-processing service, he spotted at one point a series of data-processing anomalies not of his own making. "I discovered that one of my employees was stealing from *me,*" Harlowe said. "He had been padding expense accounts on our computer, and stealing computer time so he could program and run off some accounts of his own. But I had a pretty good costing system established, and I had written an internal program that reported unit time for programs resident in that computer, and I called the guy in and told him exactly what he was doing. He turned white. That guy thought I was clairvoyant. I couldn't find it in my heart to reprimand him. After all, I was doing the same thing on a much grander scale. Also, I would rather have his gratitude than his resentment. So I worked out what I called a rational solution with him—a bonus arrangement he could draw against, so he'd have a little more ready money coming in. He was astounded by my benevolence."

Harlowe had to keep constantly on the alert to insure that his frauds were so well integrated into the produce company's computer records as to pass muster with the firm of independent auditors whose representatives came to the company offices once a year, in March or April. Usually, Harlowe said, an auditors' inspection took several days to complete. He said that the auditors were unaware that he owned the computer-service company processing the books. The general ledger was in printout form, and Harlowe made a point of being present during the audit. "When the auditors wanted some supporting detail, I would bring it," he told me. He went on, "Being present, I knew at just what stage of the audit they would leave for the night. There were certain parts of the books that I felt I would rather not have a complete audit on. So a couple of times in the course of an audit, when the auditors had gone home for the night, I would go to the data center and run off on the computer new printouts of the whole year of records under review. In the process, I would shift some accounting details—the ones I'd rather not have inspected—from the as yet unaudited part of the accounts and have the computer bury them in printouts that had already been audited. Since the auditors were working from broad totals in their separate work sheets, I kept the new total in conformity with their figures but changed the supporting details and some subtotals. Then I went back to the company office and just switched the new printouts of the year's accounts with the ones that the auditors were working on. Each time, the auditors would come in the next morning and work on an entirely new set of books without knowing it. At the end of one audit, I went out to dinner with the auditors. They complimented me on the completeness and detail and general quality of the records I was keeping. What they particularly liked was the way in which I had integrated management information into the general records. They thought that it was a comprehensive system, and they even discussed with me the possibility of using my computer applications for another of their clients, who was also in the produce business. After that dinner, I went out to my car in the restaurant parking lot and laughed until tears came down my cheeks."

As the years of successful embezzlement went on, and the total amount of money that Harlowe had diverted from the produce company's treasury approached $1 million, he began to think of pulling up stakes and moving on. "I had a very tough job at best, organizing the accounts of a company that was run by people I didn't like,"

Harlowe told me. "And when you're manipulating double accounts a job like that is even more difficult. In 1967, I decided that the time had come to stop this defalcation and to go into the next phase of my life, whatever that might be." But withdrawing from the produce company, he knew, posed some tough problems. "The principal problem was that in order to leave the job I would have to do a lot of readjusting of the computer," Harlowe said. "I would have to find a way of winding down the inflated cost figures. And I couldn't do this overnight without attracting attention. I couldn't allow the costs to drop suddenly—particularly in a period of inflation. It would take me a couple of years." Also, he said, because of some preliminary inquiries by the Internal Revenue Service, he suspected that several companies—of which the company he worked for was one—were prime candidates for investigation by I.R.S. auditors because of some of their business practices, and this prospect made him very reluctant to leave, since he would then no longer be able to manipulate the company books to keep himself out of trouble. It seemed now that the electronic dead souls that Harlowe had created had not only assumed a stubborn life of their own but were exerting an increasingly dominating force on their creator's own capacity for action.

The idea came to Harlowe that he might find a way out of his dilemma by having at least some of the defalcations revealed, but without his being blamed for them. He believed he would not be unjustified in making it appear that a couple of the principals of the produce company were themselves siphoning off money from the treasury, in order to escape taxation. "I had a unique position, in that the principals of the company were very impatient about paperwork," he explained. "They had me balance their checkbooks, pay their bills, and keep their personal bank accounts. That made it easy for me to salt their accounts, and that's what I did. I began putting checks from company accounts into their personal accounts, and from there into oblivion via dummy companies. Since I always got their bank statements, I would destroy these checks when they came back. But the transactions were recorded. I didn't do a lot of this. Just enough to suggest some possible culpability—that there was more there than met the eye."

Then Harlowe pondered how the true state of the company's finances might be discovered without his being blamed. He considered going to the chief officer and saying that he was doing so as an act of conscience. "My role would be that of the dutiful employee." But he decided against that. "Instead," he told me, "I decided to overdraw the bank account of one of my dummy companies, and deliberately call the bank's attention to the dummy company the produce company was dealing with." He had his computer turn out a check from the dummy company for an amount that the company's bank account would not cover, so as to alert the bank to the phantom nature of the company. But, to Harlowe's intense annoyance, the dummy company's bank paid no attention to the bad check. So Harlowe had the computer write another bad check, and then another. Only after about a month, when he had overdrawn the dummy account with checks amounting to $78,000, did one of the bank's officers become suspicious. The bank manager called Harlowe, who expressed puzzlement. The bank manager arranged for a

meeting with a vice-president of the produce company—
one of the people whose personal checkbooks Harlowe
happened to be manipulating. Harlowe told me he later
learned that the meeting ended in a state of confusion,
while he remained the only person who understood what
was really going on.

At that point, Harlowe told me, he calculated that the
people running the produce company—for their own reasons, connected with company finances—would be eager
to avoid any intensive examination of its financial affairs. And if by any chance they did press for a thorough
investigation, there would be enough evidence around to
divert attention from Harlowe's own culpability. But
then, as the atmosphere at his company grew tense and
suspicious, Harlowe developed apprehensions as to how
well he had really covered his tracks. He went to a lawyer
in the area who was noted for his skill in complicated
cases, told him the whole story, and paid him a fee of
$50,000 (a small portion of the funds that Harlowe had
embezzled, after all) after being assured, he said, that he
had a defensible case. Harlowe told me that, taking his
discussions with the lawyer into account, he did indeed
consider that if the produce company had him arrested
when some of the facts came out he would have a pretty
good case in court. "The principals of the company were
not entirely blameless," he said. "So far as I'm concerned
they really were trying to take money out of the business,
overstating expenses to avoid taxes. I'd be testifying as a
naïve bookkeeper. The accounting was so terribly complex that no layman juror could understand all these
computer-programming technicalities. I felt I could come
out pretty well."

But then, after the company management did sign a criminal complaint against Harlowe, and he was arrested and put on trial for grand theft, he had second thoughts about going through with this elaborate plan to shift the blame for his defalcations, and his lawyer persuaded him to plead nolo contendere. "The lawyer had it arranged, he believed, so that with the nolo plea I would get eighteen months," Harlowe said. "I thought that that wasn't so bad." Before being sentenced, he was called in for a probation-department interview. Harlowe, confident that all was settled, not only refused to tell what had become of the $1 million he had embezzled but, he admitted to me, "was pretty curt with the probation officer." In large part because of his generally uncoöperative attitude, the probation officer's presentencing report was highly unfavorable, and, in court, the judge grimly gave him not the expected eighteen months in jail but ten years in San Quentin—apparently a record sentence to date in any case of computer crime. While he was in jail, Harlowe worked his way up to become a clerk to the warden ("I was really treated more as a staff member than as an inmate"), and also taught a course in basic computer-programming techniques to fellow-prisoners.

Harlowe was released on parole in 1974. When I talked with him, he said he was on the verge of settling accounts with the I.R.S., as part of the aftermath of his embezzlement. According to Harlowe, the I.R.S. people were somewhat confounded by his case. In spite of the fact that he had admitted embezzling more than $1 million from the produce company, and in spite of the fact that embezzled funds are subject to taxes, he was allowed to settle with the I.R.S. people for only a few thousand dollars.

Harlowe explained the situation to me by saying, "At some point in my financial maneuverings, the income from the embezzlement had become income in a corporation in which I was the principal shareholder. Through various pipelines, I contributed cash from the embezzlement amounting to close to a million dollars to the corporation, and I listed this income to the corporation as though it represented sales. So in fact it was as though I had made a proper accounting of the funds for tax purposes. The I.R.S. man I dealt with found that most peculiar. He'd never come across a case before where embezzled funds had been declared—if under somewhat different colors—as income." Even so, the corporate tax paid on this sum apparently amounted to very little indeed, because Harlowe had been able to demonstrate to the government's satisfaction that the company he had established had kept losing money. How it supposedly lost it was something I couldn't get any clear idea of from Harlowe. I had the impression that the money just wafted away through a maze of intercorporate dealings and into—to use Harlowe's word—oblivion. Whatever thoughts Harlowe might have about his embezzlement, he clearly didn't have much time for the sort of remorse that seems to be sought as an ideal by sentencing judges and by probation people. He merely observed at one point that "when you get close to a computer, get really involved with it, you tend to lose track of that humaneness—you become enthralled by the numbers, you generate them endlessly, and your whole life becomes so bound up with them that you lose a qualitative sense."

Lately, Harlowe, no longer on parole, has been acting

as a data-processing consultant to a group of construction companies in northern California, for which he has written a series of programs embracing a whole range of accounting procedures, in areas from supplies to accounts payable and receivable. He told me that he also possessed a particular computer program that he had written in prison, and that he thought it had good commercial potential in the area of cost analysis. He said that he had become interested in prison reform, and added that, in part as a consequence of his prison experiences, he was occasionally in touch with some politically radical friends, some of whom had approached him for advice on taking action against computer systems as symbols of the Establishment. "These people consider themselves urban guerrillas, but they are intelligent enough to realize that violence will only bring repression," Harlowe said. "They feel that the best way to further their cause is to screw up major computer systems, such as the big credit-card outfits and the billing systems of major oil companies. They told me they were putting together a technical task force, and invited me to join it. For obvious reasons, I declined. I'm not in favor of sabotaging computers. Might be mine!"

7

Security vs. Flexibility

The accelerating incidence of computer-related crimes—particularly in the light of the continuing rapid growth of the computer industry and the present ubiquity of electronic data-processing systems—raises the question of what countermeasures can be taken within industry and government to prevent such crimes or, at least, to detect them with precision when they occur. By far the biggest manufacturer and lessor of computers is, of course, the International Business Machines Corporation, and the I.B.M. people can hardly be expected to ignore the increasing attention that the press and the public are devoting to computer crimes. I.B.M. undertook, beginning in the early 1970s, a $40 million program to examine the whole problem of data security as it applies to the computers that I.B.M. produces and to the operating systems that it designs and sells or leases. In spite of this, however, and although it is a matter of general knowledge within the industry that I.B.M. has assigned teams of specialists to examine in detail breaches of security occurring in I.B.M. systems (the company is said to have compiled a catalogue of more than 300 cases of computer crime), the I.B.M. people resolutely refuse to discuss any specifics of computer crimes that may have come to their attention. In fact, they can be brought to concede only with reluctance that the problem exists at all.

When I managed to interview John Rankine, the director of data-security programs for I.B.M., he characterized the incidence of purposeful subversion of computer systems as "minuscule." He politely declined to discuss either particular cases of computer crime of which the I.B.M. people were aware or general types of cases that the company might know about because computer crime, he told me, was not a subject that he followed in detail. Still, he did willingly discuss the overall issue of data security in computer systems, which, he said, was a fundamental one in the entire history of computer science and had to do primarily with the prevention of unintentional destruction or distortion of digitized information in the computer process. "The accountant does not want his system destroyed by the engineer, and the scientist who is working on a problem wants to protect his interim results in the computing process without having the next set of computations destroy them," Rankine said. He went on to say that his company's responsibility was to have data security as a basic design criterion, and that the issue of computer crime was actually only a very small part of the drive to achieve the integrity of computer systems as a whole. Rankine then discussed some of the procedures that his company had devised or had recommended to organizations using its computers and computer systems. In addition to tight physical security for facilities, these included such internal checks within a system to insure data security as adequate identification procedures for people communicating with the computer by way of keyboard terminals; elaborate internal audit trails built into a system, in which every significant communication between a user and a computer would be recorded; and, where confidentiality was particularly important, cryptography, or the scrambling of information. He said that, for example, in the matter of data security, to forestall the use of a terminal by someone in such a way that another terminal in a system would appear to be the one used, I.B.M. is now offering computer terminals activated by lock-and-key devices that, when the keys are turned, emit a signal identifying the terminal site to the central computer.

Other security devices in the development stage include a pen that will record, for identification purposes, not only the personal signature of a terminal user but also the dynamics involved in writing the signature out, such as the characteristic pattern of acceleration and deceleration used in forming individual strokes; and a device that will oblige the user of a terminal, before he can get a go-ahead from the computer to use it, to press his thumbprint on a special plate in a recess of the terminal for an instantaneous matching of its whorls and loops against an image stored within the computer. But, Rankine said, he didn't want to emphasize the importance of particular devices unduly, for "precautions on behalf of data security are made throughout the system." The fact is, he said, that "the data-security job will never be done—after all, there will never be a bank that absolutely can't be robbed." The main thing, he said, is to make the cost of breaching security so high that the effort involved will be discouragingly great.

In this respect, the I.B.M. people—as the result of a proposal made to computer manufacturers by the National Bureau of Standards that they develop a procedure for secure encryption of digital information—have taken the lead in constructing such a system. The procedure they have produced, after very elaborate work, has been adopted, under the name of the Data Encryption Standard, by the bureau as a required algorithm in the cryptographic handling of all federal unclassified information.

As the major manufacturer of computers and the major designer of programs to operate them, the I.B.M. organization, while obviously aware of the increasing problems of data security, is careful to place itself at a cool distance from the consequences of misuses of its equipment and systems. In a statement on data security it said, in part, "I.B.M. has developed and is continuing to develop equipment, software, and various techniques and procedures to safeguard computer information. It is the responsibility of the user to see that these data-security measures are applied as needed." Though computer-security specialists I have talked with tend to be sympathetic concerning the somewhat difficult position that I.B.M. finds itself in, particularly as the designer of computer-operating systems that may have been misused by unscrupulous employees of other corporations using the systems, they also tend to speak with a certain, though not necessarily disrespectful, skepticism of the value of some of the countermeasures against computer crime and misuse which the I.B.M. people say they have been developing under their data-security program.

Donald Adams, of the American Institute of Certified Public Accountants, who himself has a background as a computer programmer, told me that he has been unofficially "crusading" for a tightening up of what he considers to be in effect the loose design of commonly used I.B.M. and other computer systems. "The problem is that I.B.M. and other manufacturers try to make their systems so flexible that, in my view, they have made them virtually uncontrollable," Adams said. He added that it was his personal belief that in selling its systems to users I.B.M. tended to appeal to the needs of technicians rather than to what might sometimes be the best interests of top management. The flexibility of I.B.M. computer systems commonly used in business, he explained, was an attractive feature to the technicians of the user companies, especially in terms of program design, but was likely to make for systems that were relatively insecure. But top management people aren't usually aware of the lack of security that goes with flexible systems, he said, because "the management is dependent on what the technicians tell them about computer systems." And one independent computer-security consultant I talked with declared that, as far as he was concerned, most of what I.B.M. has accomplished so far in its $40 million data-security program has been essentially "to fix the little problems but not the big problems."

8

Trapdoors and Trojan Horses

To somebody looking at the problem of computer crime as a whole, one conclusion that seems reasonable is that although some of the criminal manipulators of computer systems have certainly shown ingenuity, they have not employed highly sophisticated approaches to break into and misuse computer systems without detection. In a way, this fact in itself is something of a comment on the security of most existing computer systems: the brains are presumably available to commit those sophisticated computer crimes, but the reason that advanced techniques haven't been used much may well be that they haven't been necessary.

Some glimmering of the more advanced techniques of unauthorized entry into and manipulation of computer systems which may lie ahead is perhaps observable in various exercises that have been carried out within the defense establishment for demonstration purposes, their aim being to penetrate some of the most complex and supposedly secure computer systems used by agencies of the armed forces, by civilian agencies, and by government contractors. There is, for example, the experience of a team of computer scientists from the Air Force and the MITRE Corporation—a research-and-development organization that works largely under contract to the federal government, on such projects as the National Military Command System and the Worldwide Military Command and Control System—in deliberately penetrating and manipulating the contents of what has purported to be a secure computer system. The exercises were carried out, on behalf of the Air Force, by Steven B. Lipner, an information-systems expert at the MITRE Corporation, and Lieutenant Colonel Roger R. Schell, then a computer-security specialist in the Command and Management Systems Division of the Air Force and now a student at the Air War College at Maxwell Air Force Base, in Montgomery, Alabama. The results of their efforts have been described in several Air Force and MITRE internal papers that Lipner and Schell made available to me when I visited them at the MITRE Corporation headquarters, in Bedford, Massachusetts. According to Schell, the primary aim of the exercises was not so much to derive technical insights from the penetration of a particular computer system as to demonstrate to defense officials that the penetration could be accomplished without great difficulty. In one paper that Schell and Lipner prepared for the Air Force, they put their views concerning the security of large computer systems in blunt language:

On numerous occasions, programmers have conducted formal or informal projects aimed at testing the security of operating systems by penetration—by writing programs that obtain access to information without authorization. . . . In each case, the result has been total success for the penetrators. The programmers involved in these efforts have not been "insiders" but simply competent system programmers armed with user- and (sometimes) system-level documentation for the computer and operating system under test.

Both Lipner and Schell had been studying problems in computer security since 1972, and between 1972 and 1975 they undertook a series of exercises involving the security of an advanced computer-time-sharing system called Multics, which had been developed jointly by Honeywell Incorporated and the Massachusetts Institute of Technology, partly with Defense Department funds. According to Schell, security had been a significant consideration in the design of the Multics system. It was designed to provide protection for numerous users simultaneously, and so elaborate were the checks built in to prevent unauthorized access, and to insure that users having authorized access to one level of privileged information within the computer had no way of obtaining access to a higher level, that the Multics system had been proposed by the Air Force Data Services Center at the Pentagon as a means of handling secret computerized defense information. The security precautions included a cryptographic system to encode user passwords, so as to make the passwords meaningless even if they were copied or physically stolen from the computer storage system. The exercise was carried out first on a Multics system at the Rome Air Development Center, at Griffiss Air Force Base, in New York, and then it was carried out a second time on a Multics system at M.I.T. For the purposes of these exercises, Lipner and Schell were allowed only the minimal access accorded every user. The penetration attempts were conducted from the basement of Schell's house in Concord, Massachusetts, where he installed a keyboard terminal connected to his home telephone line. He could, of course, have operated the terminal by telephone from Los Angeles or Tokyo or Moscow. Lipner and Schell told me that it took them just half an hour to determine that the Multics security system could be penetrated. It then took them two hours to write the computer program to carry out the actual penetration. Essentially, what they did, it appears, was to take advantage of the inability of a computer to make qualitative decisions. "We provided ways of making unexpected requests of the computer, and then looked to see how the computer responded to unexpected requests—things that would be nonsensical to a sensible user," Schell said. "We watched to see how the computer might respond by itself doing something unexpected." In this way, they devised a method of entering from their terminal an informational request that the computer accepted as legitimate, and, proceeding from that, they wrung from the computer compliance with a sequence of other requests.

One of the prize targets of any computer criminal attempting to penetrate a computer system has always been the master list of users' secret passwords stored within the computer's memory system—in files that are usually protected by the most elaborate security that the system can provide. Indeed, the mystique of the secret password is such that even the designers of computer systems may not fully take into account the possible reasoning of a sophisticated unauthorized user; namely, that if to get at the hidden list of secret passwords he has to break through the toughest security that the computer can provide, he would do better not to worry about the passwords at all. For if he can break into the system, he doesn't need passwords. Another barrier that the computer criminal or unauthorized user of a computer system has to cope with is that of the computer's audit trail—the internal monitoring system that can record all significant actions of the users and is supposed to provide a means of detecting and tracing unauthorized attempts to gain entry. In the Multics system, this audit mechanism was considered, even by Lipner and Schell, to be built in so securely that it was almost impossible for any attempt to obtain the passwords to escape notice. In challenging Multics, therefore, Lipner and Schell chose to ignore the audit-trail mechanism, and to allow it to record their acts as they found their way through the system. Using flaws in the operating system as entry points, they got access to essential programs and to files containing the master list of encrypted passwords. Actually, they did not consider this technically necessary, since they were confident that once they had made the initial penetration of the computer they had established the condition for gaining access to any information they wanted; they extracted the list of encrypted passwords simply by way of demonstrating what they had been doing.

Lipner and Schell didn't deign to use these passwords, since they considered themselves already well into the computer system without them. Instead, they began judiciously inserting in the computer system what are known in the business as trapdoors. In essence, a trapdoor is a special element, or anomaly, inserted in a program or system which allows the person inserting it to bypass or subvert the logical or other protective features safe-guarding the secure functioning of the system. The nature of a trapdoor is that, while it is known to and usable by a penetrator, it is unrecognized by and unknown to other users of the system—even to the audit-trail mechanism. Through the use of trapdoors, Lipner and Schell proceeded to modify parts of particular programs and the operating system itself, to their own potential advantage, present and future. In fact, they modified the system so thoroughly that even if the particular flaws which had allowed the original penetration were to be discovered and corrected, the penetrators would continue to have full access to the system.

As if all this weren't enough, Lipner and Schell also employed what people in the business sometimes refer to as the Trojan-horse technique of penetration. This technique has occasionally been used in computer crimes. It consists basically of providing the computer with apparently appropriate and acceptable information that in reality contains secret instructions for unauthorized behavior—instructions that authorized users of the system will unknowingly cause to be carried out at some future time by routinely communicating with the computer. The Trojan-horse instructions that Lipner and Schell fed into the Multics system insured that other users and the operating system itself could give them all the unauthorized information and all the control of the computer that they would ever want. As for the supposedly relentless internal-audit-trail mechanism that had recorded their entry into and progress through the computer system, Lipner and Schell, using their control of the system, simply erased from the audit system all trace of their entry. Thus, a complex computer system, which was the product of at least six years of intensive development to make it exceedingly secure, was penetrated and robbed of its internal controls in two and a half hours. Reporting on these exercises, Lipner and Schell observed, "The only sound assumption that can be made about a current computer system concerning information protection is that any program that runs on the system can access any information physically accessible to the [central] processor, and can retrieve, alter, or destroy the information as the programmer wishes."

To attempt to correct that situation, the MITRE Corporation and the Air Force have been developing an innovative system that Schell calls a "security kernel," whose use they say can vastly improve the security of data in computer systems, and Honeywell has since claimed that it has used such a kernel to make significant improvements in the security of the Multics system.

While much of the information stored in the Multics system that Lipner and Schell succeeded in penetrating would be regarded by users of the system as confidential in nature, none of it had any government-security classification. If it had been thus classified, the penetration of the system would obviously have had even greater significance. However, an exercise carried out by three computer scientists at the Naval Research Laboratory, in Washington, D.C., against an advanced computer system used by the armed forces did involve a large amount of classified information, as well as some that was unclassified. The target of this exercise was the executive, or controlling, system employed to run a Sperry Rand

Univac 1108 computer for military purposes. The executive system of the Univac was meant to process simultaneously a great number of programs with different levels of security protection, and was considered by its designers to be highly secure and complex. Indeed, a programmers' reference manual issued by the Univac people declared, concerning the system's soundness in respect to any possible intentional or unintentional invasion, "The Executive System has unique features that automatically guarantee absolute protection." The exercise was carried out by David Stryker, Dr. John Shore, and Stanley Wilson, of the Naval Research Laboratory. Because of the stringent physical-security precautions that the armed forces take on behalf of their computer systems, the men attempting the penetration of the Univac 1108 operated not from a remote telephone-connected terminal but from a terminal "hard wired" to the computer; that is, one connected in what was essentially a closed-circuit system.

When I talked with Dr. Shore at the N.R.L., he explained the nature of the exercise and discussed with me a declassified copy of an official report on it, written by Stryker and entitled "Subversion of a 'Secure' Operating System." Dr. Shore was unequivocal on the subject of complete computer security. "If you give someone who knows about computer systems enough time and unrestricted access, he'll find a way to defeat the existing controls," he said. He observed that the operating system of a large, advanced-model computer, which acts as a master-control program and allocates the resources of the computer to the tasks required of it, is so complex and contains so many instructions that it simply cannot be comprehended by a single person. For example, the number of instructions in the executive system of the Univac 1108 is about half a million, and that figure, even though it is enormous, is a good deal smaller than the totals in certain other operating systems. (One of the operating systems designed for the I.B.M. S/370 computer, I found out from the I.B.M. people, contains about six million instructions; if these were run off on computer-printout sheets, their bulk would be equivalent to one continuous instruction-filled sheet at least fifteen miles long.) A consequence of all this complexity, Dr. Shore said, is that any knowledgeable person attempting to penetrate a supposedly secure computer begins with an advantage, in that he has to find only one significant flaw in order to start working his way into the system, whereas the designers of a system are theoretically afforded no leeway at all in their attempts to make it secure.

Dr. Shore said that the exercise to penetrate the Univac 1108 system by the N.R.L. team took place in late 1973 and early 1974. The particular system against which the exercise was aimed had been modified to improve its security. For example, some of the classified material stored within the computer had been encrypted, and, as a consequence of the design of the system, could be made available to users only under strict security conditions—including, of course, proper identification of each user. In addition to these precautions, the computer system had been given other special modifications in order to increase its security. The three experts involved in the test were allowed only unclassified and unprivileged access to the computer, from a basement terminal. Their specific aim was to demonstrate the inability of the Univac operating system to prevent access to certain information by unauthorized users. Their procedure in breaking through the "absolute protection" supposedly afforded users by the Univac 1108 appears to have been similar in some respects to that of Schell and Lipner in penetrating the Multics, for it involved taking advantage of flaws and inserting trapdoors in the logic of the Univac 1108. However, what the N.R.L. experts exploited was not the existence of "bugs" in the executive program—although these certainly existed—but rather features resulting from oversights in the design of the executive program. The details of the exercise are complex. (For those readers interested in its technical aspects, see excerpts from the Stryker report, previously alluded to, in Appendix 3.) But what the intruders did, in effect, was to modify certain programs that were shared by many users despite a supposed guarantee against such modifications. As a result, a subsequent user of the now modified shared program "fell through a trapdoor," as Dr. Shore put it, which enabled the N.R.L. team to take control and impersonate that subsequent user. When they had succeeded in doing this, they had access to all the information belonging to subsequent users of the penetrated shared system. They were then able to copy classified information that had been stored in an encrypted file onto their own computer tapes, and in the copying process the Univac 1108 decrypted the classified information. They erased virtually all traces of their entry into and subsequent ravages of the system as recorded in the internal-audit mechanism, and were able with impunity to impersonate legitimate users with classified access rights.

Using only thirteen seconds of computer time in a typical subversion of the Univac 1108, they were able to copy all data belonging to other users of the penetrated shared program for a full eight hours or so. During that period, they possessed effective control over a large amount of the data in the entire computer system. "We could have selectively rewritten any of this information or selectively erased it," Dr. Shore told me. They extracted so much information from the computer that, he said, "we found we had an information-pollution problem on our hands." They had to write a computer program of their own to sort out the more significant parts of the information that the computer kept disgorging. Their choice of material amounted to between a million and two million words of text, classified and unclassified. And, as a final insult, the computer time during which the stolen information kept pouring out was billed to other users; the only computer time billed to the N.R.L. team was the thirteen seconds it took them to subvert the system. (Sperry Rand has pointed out, however, that it has introduced modifications in the design of the Univac programming system so as to improve its security.)

If these men had attacked this particular defense computer system with hostile intent, the results could clearly have been devastating. And yet Dr. Shore and his colleagues at the N.R.L. are convinced, after thorough investigation, that by prevailing standards the staff at this particular site did a "good job" in modifying a standard commercial computer operating system in order to provide better security for users. Whether in the military, in government, or in business the designers of currently contemplated computer systems seem no more able to promise absolute solutions to problems of data security than chess players are able to foresee games in which White can never be beaten. And in the meantime, nobody knows what Trojan-horse programs may be lying in wait in computer systems until, at the appropriate signal, they spill out in acts of disruption and pillage, or what electronic dead souls may be flitting within the recesses of a system until, at the direction of some intent Tchi-tchikov at a keyboard terminal, they are mustered into ghostly but immensely exploitable legions.

APPENDIXES

Appendix 1

Proposed Legislation to Control Computer Crime

From an explanatory statement made to the United States Senate on June 27, 1977, by Senator Abraham Ribicoff, of Connecticut, in introducing the Federal Computer Systems Protection Act of 1977, of which he has been the principal sponsor:

The legislation would impose heavy prison terms and stiff fines for electronic burglars who use computers and computer technology to steal or manipulate information, financial instruments, and other property.

The bill would make it a crime to misuse the computer systems of the federal government, certain financial institutions, and other entities involved in interstate commerce.

Because of a growing national dependence on computers, the opportunities for white-collar crime in this area are becoming great with little chance for prosecution under existing law.

If adopted, this bill would be the first law enacted by the Congress aimed directly at controlling crime by computer or computer-related crime. Present federal criminal law, as reflected in title 18 of the United States Code, contains some 40 sections which the government can use to combat computer-related crime. But all 40 of the statutes were written to combat abuses other than computer crimes and, as such, federal prosecutors have been handicapped because they have had to construct their cases on laws that did not envision the technical aspects of computer crime.

The measure is a result of a year-long inquiry, begun May 10, 1976, conducted by the Senate Governmental Affairs Committee.

As chairman, and with the concurrence of Senator Percy, the ranking minority member, I directed the release on February 2, 1977, of a staff report, "Computer Security in Federal Programs," a 130,000-word document that demonstrated evidence of:

1. The government's inability to adequately secure its 10,000 computers against fraud, compromise, and physical assault. This lack of adequate security is especially evident in those government computers which handle the distribution of public funds and those which hold economically valuable and privacy data;

2. Weaknesses in government procedures for predicting the integrity of its computer personnel; and

3. A concern on the part of federal law enforcement and prosecutorial officials that the U.S. Code, title 18, should be amended to strengthen the government's ability to prosecute computer crime.

It was noted in the committee staff report, for example,

that a major computer-crime conviction had been won in one well-known case only because the perpetrator had used a telephone line to penetrate the computer system of a federal contractor across state lines. Had the telephone been used intrastate rather than interstate, federal prosecutors said, the Wire Fraud Statute (18 USC 1343) under which the indictment was brought may have been inadequate. In the same case, a part of the indictment was dismissed because electromagnetic impulses which transmitted valuable data were determined not to be "property" as defined in the Interstate Transportation of Stolen Property Statute (18 USC 2314).

In another attempted prosecution, the government lost the case because of definitional difficulties in establishing whether checks issued by a computer on the basis of fraudulent or manipulated data were forgeries.

The bill we are introducing would amend title 18 of the U.S. Code in such a way as to make virtually all unauthorized use of federal computers and computers used in interstate commerce a federal offense punishable by as much as 15 years in prison or $50,000 fine, or both.

There would be no requirement that telephones or other forms of illicit computer penetration across state lines be used in order to qualify the act as a federal crime. The bill is further intended to ease the jurisdictional and evidentiary burdens posed by computer technology on federal prosecutors and law enforcement personnel.

This bill represents an important step forward in combating crime by computers.

The computer has meant progress in our society almost everywhere—from our ability to predict weather to our ability to detect potential health problems.

But the computer, because it has become such an essential aspect of our financial world—both in the private sector and in government—has also become vulnerable to criminal penetration. Another serious threat is the potential compromise and misuse of vast quantities of data on the private lives of individuals currently stored in the computer systems of the federal government and private industry.

Crime by computer is relatively new. But when it strikes it is not shy. Violators, with even a limited amount of technical knowledge, can literally steal hundreds of thousands of dollars, either from computer check-writing systems or by directing the computer to divert valuable data or costly equipment.

Our committee investigation revealed that the government has been hampered in its ability to prosecute computer crime. The reason is that our laws, primarily as embodied in title 18, have not kept current with the rapidly growing and changing computer technology.

Consequently, while prosecutors could, and often did, win convictions in crime-by-computer cases, they were forced to base their charges on laws that were written for purposes other than computer crime.

Prosecutors are forced to "shoe horn" their cases into already existing laws—when it is more appropriate for them to have a statute relating directly to computer abuses.

This bill will provide the needed corrective action. My committee staff, consulting with Justice Department officials, computer security scientists, and persons expert and actively involved in the criminal justice system, concluded that this measure, if adopted by the Congress will have applicability in virtually every computer-crime case not already adequately covered by an existing law.

This bill is specifically designed to give federal prosecutors a weapon against the four main categories of computer crime. They are:

1. the introduction of fraudulent records or data into the computer system;

2. the unauthorized use of computer-related facilities;

3. the alteration or destruction of information or files; and

4. the stealing, whether by electronic means or otherwise, of money, financial instruments, property, services, or valuable data.

Computer technology, which has produced enormous benefits for mankind, has also produced great potential for the sophisticated white-collar criminal. The simple fact as demonstrated in the staff report is that computer technology has created vulnerability to white-collar crime. This bill is designed to provide criminal sanctions at all points where computer operations are targets for criminals.

There are five key stages in a sophisticated computer system, and each stage of operation is vulnerable to a particular method of criminal attack. The first and most important stage is translation of data into computer language or input, where the data is placed on card readers or magnetic tapes. At this stage criminals can introduce false data into the computer so that key documents could be removed and fraudulent records inserted. A criminal or a criminal group with access to this stage of operation could manipulate the computer with introduction of false data, and it might be years before anyone discovers the fraud.

Computer programming is the second stage of operation and occurs when the computer is supplied with a logical sequence of instructions for the solution of problems. The computer then responds in a manner dictated by the program. Programs are easily modified, destroyed, or stolen and sold to a competitor.

The third stage involves the computer's brain, known as the central processing unit (CPU). The CPU, which contains the operating system software, guides the computer and directs it to perform the necessary functions following the instructions in the program and is susceptible to various forms of electronic penetration and manipulation. Destruction of the CPU could stop computer operation and be disastrous to a government agency, industry, or company with most of its records computerized.

Once data is received from the CPU, it is translated into an intelligible form called output—the fourth stage of the operation. Output is vulnerable to theft. Criminals at this stage could steal confidential data, such as privacy information or trade secrets. The computer systems of government agencies, financial institutions, and others contain voluminous confidential data on firms and individuals; theft of such data could easily lead to blackmail or even be sold on a black market.

The final stage of the operation, communication, involves the transmission of output to other computers and/or users. The computer is vulnerable at this stage to electronic penetration. Initially, the information will be transmitted by telephone circuits, which can be tapped.

The main section of this bill makes it a federal crime to

"access" a computer for the purpose of perpetrating fraud or obtaining money, property, or service under false or fraudulent pretenses. It should be made clear that the term "access" specifically includes within its meaning as defined in the bill all forms of unauthorized or clandestine penetration of a computer, computer system, or computer networks. These penetrations include but are not necessarily limited to:

1. Wiretapping which is gaining access to a system via direct connection to a communication line or part of the central system.

2. Radiation which is passive eavesdropping without direct connection. It siphons data from a system by detecting acoustic or electromagnetic signals emanating from a computer or component.

3. Artifice or "trapdoor entry" which is the intentional introduction of a clandestine code into a system to be used later for subversion from within. It is created by unscrupulous programmers and designers. An artifice can be implanted at the time the system is implemented or during subsequent modification; it can also be implanted by a successful penetration.

4. Impersonation which is unauthorized activity carried out by performing as a legitimate user or device such as using someone else's user identification, code and/or password to gain access to the system.

All phases of computer operations need to be made more secure from criminal penetration but all the physical security precautions in the world will be of little use if they are not accompanied by adequate personnel procedures to reduce the possibility of employment of dishonest persons. Dishonest employees who themselves engage in computer crime or engage in collusion with criminals on the outside pose the biggest threat to government and business. Computer criminals are the most sophisticated of all white-collar criminals. They currently operate in an environment and under conditions in which the successful detection and prosecution of their crimes is very difficult. When they are apprehended and convicted, all too often the sentences they receive are extraordinarily light. It is for this reason that I attach great importance to the penalty provisions of this bill.

Under terms of this bill, a federal judge may, in his discretion, depending on the severity of the crime, impose jail terms of 15 years and fines up to $50,000 on computer thieves.

It is my hope that these increased penalties, unprecedented in federal criminal law for white-collar crime, will deter the potential computer thief and at the same time pose a warning to all white-collar criminals that the Congress of the United States sees white-collar crime as a threat to our society which should be dealt with in a manner befitting the crime.

It is time to tell criminals who use computer terminals, fountain pens, and phony stock certificates to rob millions of dollars that their corrosive activities will not be tolerated.

This bill also places particular emphasis on the prosecution of crimes against the computer systems of banks and other financial institutions which are insured or regulated by the federal government. Today, financial institutions are heavily dependent on computers which process and record billions of dollars in financial transactions daily. If present trends continue, however, banks and other financial institutions will become more dependent on computers in the future. As Electronic Fund

Transfer Systems are perfected and implemented, more computers, terminals, wires, data banks, and operators will be employed to operate these intricate and complex systems of recordkeeping. Electronic Fund Transfer Systems involve the use of communication and computer networks to relay, process, and store fund transfer information. They may involve transferring funds from a buyer's account to the account of a seller or from an employer to an employee.

A national Electronic Fund Transfer System could supplant the present paper-exchange system so that paper currency or stock certificates as we now know them would play an insignificant role in transactions or even become obsolete.

The beginnings of a national EFTS can be witnessed today. Computers with multiprocessing capability and high-speed mass memory are in operation, providing a basis for at least a regional EFTS. Taking advantage of this technology, several automated clearinghouses appeared in the early 1970s. Under the present system, banks maintain clearing balances on one another or on a common bank such as the Federal Reserve Bank. Because transactions are processed electronically, the cumbersome process of hand-sorting and paper and pen work has been eliminated; in addition, the automated clearinghouse rapidly adjusts balances. Automated clearinghouses are a logical starting point for the development of a national EFTS.

The "point-of-sale" system represents a more sophisticated step in the development of an EFTS. Under a point of sale the buyer can pay for his purchase without the intervention of currency. As in an EFTS the buyer gives the store clerk an identification card to insert in a terminal linked to a bank's computer; the purchase price is then transferred from the buyer's account to the store account. If the store does not maintain an account at the bank, the transfer process takes place as it presently does through some form of clearinghouse.

The automated clearinghouse and the point-of-sale systems are rudimentary compared to the sophisticated and elaborate technology required to link up a national EFTS. A national system will rely on thousands of computers, millions of terminals and millions of miles of wire with thousands of technicians and computer operators needed to man it. It can totally displace ink. The work-horse of EFTS is the computer, and the technology which makes the system possible also makes it vulnerable to criminal attack.

There are at least four areas where the protective criminal-law sanctions of the bill I am introducing today will apply to EFTS. They are:

1. unauthorized access to a customer's account by means of the theft or reproduction of an access "key," such as the plastic card, given the customer;

2. unauthorized access to accounts by personnel manning access terminals, such as the store employees operating the supermarket remote deposit-withdrawal system;

3. unauthorized access to communication lines between remote terminals and information storage areas, such as a financial institution's central processing unit, in short, wiretapping; and

4. unauthorized access at the central processing unit site by employees or outsiders.

In addition, I wish to make it clear that nothing in this legislation is intended to reduce, restrict, or supersede existing statutes and nothing in this legislation reduces existing investigative authority of any law enforcement or national security agency under existing law or duly authorized practices.

The Senate Governmental Affairs Committee investigation, which led to the staff report, "Computer Security in Federal Programs," and this bill have been studied by the Office of Management and Budget (OMB). Issues raised in the staff report have been examined by OMB, which has overall fiscal and policy control of all automatic data processing (ADP) operations in the executive branch.

As a result of the attention focused on computer security by the committee inquiry, OMB is in the process of revising its government-wide regulations affecting computer security. These regulations, which are contained in OMB Circular A-71, are being strengthened and upon completion of their revision will be made available to the public.

Not affected by the revised OMB Circular A-71, or by this bill, is another problem raised by the Senate committee's investigation—that problem being the growing and widespread multiple-filer schemes in which violators create bogus tax forms, file them with the Internal Revenue Service, and are then sent by computers sizeable refunds, ranging in amounts from $500 to $500,000.

Such schemes are already clearly against the law and neither IRS nor the Justice Department needs a new statute to control them. What is required, IRS officials have indicated to the committee, is an improved system for detection and such a system is being implemented, IRS officials say.

Appendix 2

Computer-Related Crimes in Federal Programs

Excerpts from a special report submitted to Congress by the Comptroller General of the United States, General Accounting Office, April 1976.

DIGEST

Computer systems have added a new dimension for potential crime. Computer-related crimes in federal programs are cause for growing concern.

Information on computer-related crimes is difficult to obtain, because the crimes frequently are not classified as such by investigative agencies. Even so, GAO has learned of crimes or other incidents [in federal programs] resulting in losses of over $2 million. In addition to the dollar loss to the government, some crimes violate the privacy of individuals about whom computerized records are kept.

Contrary to widespread belief, most of these acts have

been committed by persons who possess limited technical knowledge of computers—that is, by users of automatic data-processing systems rather than by persons with more technical knowledge such as programmers, operators, or analysts.

GAO found that management controls over the systems involved in crimes were inadequate....

THE NATURE OF GOVERNMENT COMPUTER CRIMES

A wide variety of computer-related crimes in all levels of government has been discovered. Most have been committed by persons who possess only limited technical knowledge of computers; that is, users of ADP [Automatic Data Processing] systems rather than persons with more technical knowledge such as programmers, operators, or analysts. Of the 69 cases in our files, at least 50 were committed by system users, not ADP personnel.

A Stanford Research Institute (SRI) report prepared for us notes that, although sophisticated computer crimes are the ones that get publicity, most criminals discovered so far used unsophisticated methods. Moreover, most committed their crimes within their own work environments.

Our review of government cases shows results similar to those in the Stanford Research report.

What Kinds of Crimes Are Occurring?

We can best illustrate the varied types of crimes by giving some examples of cases gathered from agency records.

The majority of cases—about 62 percent—involved

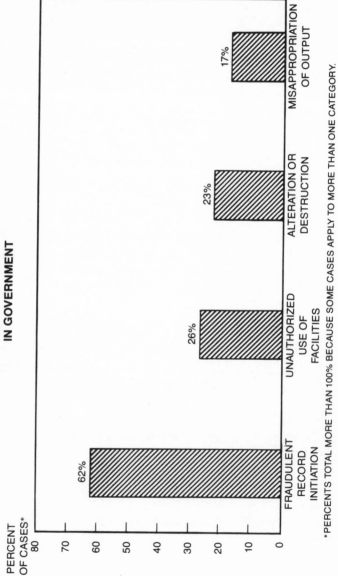

TYPES OF COMPUTER-RELATED CRIMES
IN GOVERNMENT

PERCENT
OF CASES*

*PERCENTS TOTAL MORE THAN 100% BECAUSE SOME CASES APPLY TO MORE THAN ONE CATEGORY.

persons preparing fraudulent input to computer-based systems. (See chart.) Several variations of this method have been discovered.

Supply systems are particularly vulnerable to fraudulent input. In one case, a perpetrator used a computer terminal to ascertain the location and availability of items desired by outside conspirators. Once he located those items, the perpetrator caused the system to prepare fraudulent requisitioning documents. Then he used the documents to obtain the items he wanted, took the items from the installation, and sold them to the outside parties. Although the total amount of property stolen through computerized supply systems cannot easily be determined, the value of one such theft in our case files was about $53,000. Another loss of over $300,000 was averted when discrepancies were discovered accidentally and the material recovered.

Many cases discovered to date in which the individuals involved prepared fraudulent input involve systems that make direct payments to individuals or businesses. These include fraudulent payroll, social welfare, and compensation transactions as well as payments for nonexistent goods and services. For example:

—A government employee who had helped automate an accounting system introduced fraudulent payment vouchers into the system. The computer could not recognize that the transactions were fraudulent and issued checks payable to fictitious companies set up by the employee and his accomplices. These checks were sent directly to banks where the conspirators had opened accounts for the companies. The criminals then withdrew the funds from the accounts. Officials estimated the government may have paid this employee and his accomplices $100,000 for goods that had never been delivered.

—A supervisory clerk responsible for entering claim transactions to a computer-based social welfare system found she could introduce fictitious claims on behalf of accomplices and they would receive the benefits. She was able to process over $90,000 in claims (authorities believe it might have been up to $250,000) before she was discovered through an anonymous telephone tip.

Another type of act, which has occurred in several agencies, is the unauthorized use of computers by ADP personnel. An engineer who was no longer employed at a computer installation managed to continue using the equipment for his own purposes. Before he was discovered, he had used over $4,000 worth of computer time. At another installation, a programmer used a self-initiated training program to obtain use of his agency's computer system. But instead of working on the training exercise, he was developing his own computer programs which he hoped to sell.

Computer-related crime does not always lead to direct monetary losses. The manager of a nonfederal computer center processing personal information was able to steal some of this data and sell it to outside parties who were not authorized to use it. Although the government did not lose any money, the privacy of individuals whose data records were involved was violated, and this is of concern in protecting the privacy of personal information.

For convenience, we have categorized the methods used to commit known government computer crimes.

Category 1—initiation of fraudulent records (input)

Includes such crimes as deliberately falsifying input documents or records, entering counterbalancing transactions, and falsifying claims by reuse of supporting documents previously processed.

Category 2—unauthorized or inappropriate use of facilities and supplies

Includes developing salable programs on organizations' computers, doing commercial service-bureau-type work for outsiders on organizations' computers, using remote terminals for personal benefit, and duplicating magnetic files and selling them.

Category 3—processing alteration or destruction

Includes such crimes as sabotage or altering information recorded in the files affecting pay, promotion, or assignment and bypassing existing controls to enter unauthorized changes. These crimes could be done by operators intervening to perform unauthorized processing, resulting in gain to the operator or his accomplice, or by programmers altering computer programs.

Category 4—misappropriation of output

Includes such crimes as misappropriating returned checks and eliminating or altering notices designed to provide controls and balances.

[The chart on page 142 shows the percentage of cases in GAO files which relate to each of these categories.]

Why Do These Crimes Occur?

In every case we reviewed in detail, the incidents were directly traceable to weaknesses in system controls.

These weaknesses were the result of deficient systems designs, improper implementation of controls by operating personnel, or a combination of both. Moreover, the weaknesses were in basic management controls, such as separation of duties and physical access control over facilities.

The primary reason weaknesses in system controls existed was that management failed to recognize the importance of controlling systems. This lack of emphasis affected both the way systems were designed and the extent to which operating personnel enforced controls.

Managers can use internal auditors as an important part of management control. But agencies' internal audit groups vary greatly in how they review ADP systems. Often the auditors were not aware of crimes that demonstrated weaknesses in internal control systems.

The following chapters explain the types of control weaknesses which have been exploited, the importance of management emphasis on controlling systems, and the roles played by auditors in the cases we reviewed.

CRIMINALS EXPLOITED WEAKNESSES IN BASIC
MANAGEMENT CONTROLS

System controls are designed to protect the assets of an organization. Thus, it is not surprising that, in committing their crimes, perpetrators take advantage of system control weaknesses. What may be surprising is that the weaknesses exploited are mostly basic management controls long recognized as being necessary to insure proper operations.

The most common weaknesses which have been exploited in our cases were in (1) separation of duties and (2) physical control over facilities and supplies. Sometimes these weaknesses are due to poorly designed systems, but in seven of the twelve cases we reviewed in detail, controls or procedures existed but were not enforced by operating personnel.

Inadequate Separation of Duties and Poor Physical Controls Are the Most Common Weaknesses

Using computers compresses activities into fewer hands. Under such circumstances, management should critically evaluate the amount of control any one individual exercises over processing steps. In seven of the twelve cases, inadequate separation of duties was a major weakness contributing to the perpetrators' successes.

In one social benefit program, the perpetrator was a system user, a representative responsible for certifying the eligibility of benefit recipients. But he also prepared data to be put into the ADP system for controlling and issuing negotiable coupons. Although the system identified some discrepancies, no one investigated or reconciled the discrepancies. Using his position in the organization to his own advantage, he processed a series of fraudulent claims, causing coupons to be sent to accomplices not eligible to receive them. The coupons were then redeemed by accomplices. No one reviewed the validity of transactions initiated by this clerk, and he did not even have to prepare backup source documents to support the fraudulent claims.

ADP personnel also can take advantage of too much

concentrated authority and responsibility. One of our cases involved the manager of a small nonfederal computer center. This person had authority to establish procedures at the center, revise those procedures at his own discretion, and circumvent established operational controls with little or no review by supervisors or system users. He used his position to sell information on private citizens to special interest groups which paid him an estimated $48,000 for that information. As previously stated, this violated the privacy of persons whose records he sold.

Another common weakness is poor physical control of facilities and supplies. Some examples of these weaknesses include unauthorized access to computer rooms, unauthorized use of terminals, unrestricted access to computer tape files, and free access to documents authorizing transactions. Such weaknesses led directly to improprieties in five of the twelve cases.

MANAGEMENT DOES NOT PLACE SUFFICIENT EMPHASIS ON CONTROLLING SYSTEMS

Primary responsibility for control of operations rests with top management—a legal requirement in federal agencies as well as a tenet of sound management practice. Our review showed that managers often do not place sufficient emphasis on controlling systems, and this lack of emphasis results in poorly designed or inadequately enforced controls. This presents increased opportunities to criminals.

**Management Placed Priority on
Making Systems Operational Rather
Than on Controlling Them**

Managers of organizations involved in many of the twelve cases we reviewed had primarily emphasized making their systems operational; control was not emphasized.

In one case involving a social compensation system, automatic data-processing personnel told us their organization's processing was built around second-generation computers and had no fraud-oriented controls built in. When they converted to more modern equipment, the system was not redesigned because of pressure to get the new computers running. An employee submitted fraudulent claims to this system, and the system sent her checks totaling over $15,000.

Another case involved a contractor ordering government-furnished material for approved contracts directly through a government supply system, using a remote terminal device. No controls existed to insure that the material ordered (by type or quantity) was appropriate to a given contract, and the contractor requisitioned over $300,000 worth of material to which it was not entitled and for which it would not have paid. In designing the system, officials had emphasized speeding up the requisition process; they considered time more critical than controls that might delay delivery.

Management should give attention to controlling systems as well as to implementing them. Managers should continuously assess operations to insure a proper balance between performance of systems and control over assets.

IMPROVEMENT NEEDED IN AUDITS OF SYSTEM
CONTROLS

Internal auditing is an important part of the management control function. It complements other elements of
management control, and it provides independent judg-
ment on the ways managers have carried out their responsibilities.

Our Standards for Audit of Governmental Organizations, Programs, Activities, and Functions require
evaluations of systems of internal control.

Proper auditing of system controls and procedures can
detect weaknesses that facilitate criminal activity and
can help discourage potential criminals. But federal
agencies' internal audit groups vary greatly in how they
review automatic data-processing systems. In nine of the
twelve cases we studied, auditors had not reviewed controls in the systems involved. To plan their work properly, audit staffs should be made aware of criminal activity which resulted from weaknesses in controls. But often
they are not.

Proper Audits Can Detect Weaknesses That Lead to Crimes

The auditor's responsibility in detecting fraud is the subject of current controversy. However, adequate reviews of
internal controls can and do help detect weaknesses that
facilitate crimes, thus helping management prevent
them. Audits or special reviews in 13 of the 69 cases in
our files—about 19 percent—actually did result in the
discovery of improprieties.

Auditors reviewing system controls in two of the cases
identified and reported weaknesses in them. In both

cases, the auditors made recommendations to correct the weaknesses, but in each case management action was inadequate. The weaknesses continued to exist, and the criminals took advantage of them.

Audits of Controls Had Not Been Made

We found wide variations in the approaches federal agencies' internal audit staffs have taken to review ADP systems. Some auditors become involved during system development, and some do not. Use of specific audit techniques, such as test decks, retrieval packages, and specially written computer audit programs, varies widely. Most agencies believe their audit staffs should have knowledge about various aspects of ADP—such as design, operation, and controls—but the auditors' own estimates of their abilities to address these areas show great differences.

No internal audits of system controls had been made in five of the twelve cases. In four other cases, investigative officials, not auditors, had reviewed specific systems controls as they related to crimes already detected. Even in the one agency in which auditors' reviews had revealed system weaknesses, federal officials responsible for the audits stated that the programs involved were so large that the agency did not have the resources to make onsite inspections or followup reviews on recommendations. They stated they had to do much of their work through correspondence and meetings. They did not assure themselves management had taken appropriate action on reported deficiencies.

Although we cannot say that audits of controls would have detected or prevented all 69 incidents, such audits are recognized as an important part of good overall management control. Some agency officials told us of specific plans to review systems procedures and controls, and some had been reviewing them regularly. Others had not, and overall we found audits of controls either inadequate or ineffective.

Auditors Should Be Informed of Criminal Activity Indicating Control Weaknesses

Information on frauds and unusual irregularities should be made available to us and to others in the agencies who may legitimately inquire into them. This is pointed out in title 7 of our Manual for Guidance of Federal Agencies. But agency internal auditors often had not been informed about computer-related crimes so they could consider their effect on audit procedures. In several of the cases we reviewed, auditors told us our inquiry was the first time they had heard of the crimes.

For internal auditors to be responsive to needs of management and the organization, they should have information necessary to develop adequate work procedures. Sharing information on criminal activity involving systems problems at various organizational levels is necessary to insure good planning of audits.

CONCLUSIONS AND RECOMMENDATIONS

The number of computer-related crimes in government as well as in the private sector is cause for concern about how well systems are being controlled. The dollar values of government cases we know about are not as large as those in some crimes in private businesses, but we cannot be sure whether factors in government systems prevent larger losses or whether we simply have not uncovered larger crimes.

It is clear the potential for computer-related crimes exists, especially since reliance on the computer is increasing. We know that weaknesses in the design and the execution of controls in automatic data-processing systems make it easier to commit crimes. We have evidence that security surrounding federal computer installations and applications is about the same as that in the private sector, and in our own reviews of federal agencies' systems, we continue to find weaknesses in design and enforcement of controls.

Computers have added a new dimension to the potential for crimes. They can make crimes harder to detect because computer-based systems usually provide fewer written records of transactions. These systems naturally concentrate processing in fewer hands and make proper separation of duties more difficult to achieve. The concentration of asset information in easily changed form increases the potential size of each loss.

As a result of these characteristics, there should be a more systematic approach to preventing and detecting crimes in computer-based systems than was necessary for manual systems. This means better internal control and more effort to see that the system is operating as designed.

Although government-wide standards on internal controls and on audits of internal controls have existed for several years, heads of federal organizations need to insure that adequate controls are designed into computer-based systems serving them and that those controls are functioning properly....

Appendix 3

Penetration of a Univac Computer

Subversion of a "Secure" Operating System

The multiprogramming capabilities of the Executive System imply that many unrelated programs may be residing in main storage at the same time. Infringement of privacy in such a mixture is highly probable, especially in cases where debugging tasks are executing.... To combat the invasion, intentional or unintentional, the Executive System has unique features that automatically guarantee absolute program protection.

Programmers Reference Manual
Univac Publication UP-4144,
Rev. 3, p. 2–20

INTRODUCTION

As the practice of online maintenance of data on multi-access computer systems has snowballed, the importance

SECURITY CLASSIFICATION OF THIS PAGE *(When Data Entered)*

REPORT DOCUMENTATION PAGE		READ INSTRUCTIONS BEFORE COMPLETING FORM
1. REPORT NUMBER NRL Memorandum Report 2821	2. GOVT ACCESSION NO.	3. RECIPIENT'S CATALOG NUMBER
4. TITLE *(and Subtitle)* SUBVERSION OF A "SECURE" OPERATING SYSTEM (U)		5. TYPE OF REPORT & PERIOD COVERED Interim report
		6. PERFORMING ORG. REPORT NUMBER
7. AUTHOR*(s)* David J. Stryker		8. CONTRACT OR GRANT NUMBER*(s)*
9. PERFORMING ORGANIZATION NAME AND ADDRESS Naval Research Laboratory Washington, D.C. 20375		10. PROGRAM ELEMENT, PROJECT, TASK AREA & WORK UNIT NUMBERS NRL Prob. 54B02-08 Task No. 351502-74-01
11. CONTROLLING OFFICE NAME AND ADDRESS Naval Electronic Systems Command (ELEX 5301)		12. REPORT DATE June 1974
		13. NUMBER OF PAGES 18
14. MONITORING AGENCY NAME & ADDRESS*(if different from Controlling Office)*		15. SECURITY CLASS. *(of this report)* UNCLASSIFIED
		15a. DECLASSIFICATION/DOWNGRADING SCHEDULE AGDS-Dec. 31, 1974

16. DISTRIBUTION STATEMENT *(of this Report)*

Distribution limited to U.S. Government Agencies only; test and evaluation; June 1974. Other requests for this document must be referred to the Director, Naval Research Laboratory, Washington, D.C. 20375.

17. DISTRIBUTION STATEMENT *(of the abstract entered in Block 20, if different from Report)*

18. SUPPLEMENTARY NOTES

19. KEY WORDS *(Continue on reverse side if necessary and identify by block number)*

Operating Systems, Security

20. ABSTRACT *(Continue on reverse side if necessary and identify by block number)*

(U) This Memorandum Report describes the successful, covert subversion of a Univac 1108 Exec VIII operating system at a facility where classified and unclassified data were simultaneously resident on the system, and speculates on those aspects of the supervisor design that make penetration possible. Recommendations are made to remedy some of the faults of Exec VIII, and guidelines for the development of other operating systems are discussed.

DD $_{1\ JAN\ 73}^{FORM}$ **1473** EDITION OF 1 NOV 65 IS OBSOLETE
S/N 0102-014-6601

i

of data integrity has been recognized. The operating systems (OS) of multi-access computers normally have complete control over all system facilities, so that a breach of OS security can result in the dissemination, destruction, or modification of all data stored in the system. Any software serviced by the OS is as insecure as the OS itself.

Ideally, one would like to require that OS's be absolutely secure in the sense that they never permit access to a user's data without that user's permission. A realistic requirement is that the cost of penetration exceed the value of the data gained from penetration.

The Department of Defense maintains classified data on its computer systems, and believes that the cost of penetration should be correspondingly higher than is normally required on commercial systems. When several classes of users (e.g., Unclassified, Confidential, Secret, etc.) maintain data online on the same computer system, the term "Multilevel Security (MLS) System" is often used to describe the corresponding OS requirement. If an OS were completely secure, it would protect each user's data from all other users, and the division of user capabilities by the user's level of classification would be unnecessary. It is a much less stringent requirement to provide a MLS system than it is to provide a secure OS, which guarantees the data integrity of each user.

We believe that penetration of most large OS's can be performed at very low costs. However, because there are few well-documented examples of such penetration, there is a false sense of security among system managers, many of whom believe that holes in their systems exist in theory, but are in practice nearly impossible to exploit.

The Naval Research Laboratory (NRL) has performed

several tests of MLS systems; this Memorandum Report describes one aspect of a test of a MLS system operating on the Univac 1108. The OS tested was a version of the level 31 Exec VIII that was modified on site to improve its security in an MLS environment. Users were assured that their classified data was protected adequately. However, since no basic design features of Exec VIII were changed, our penetration was merely somewhat more difficult than it would have been in the case of a standard Exec VIII.

Our penetration of Exec VIII was based on the insertion of "trapdoors" in sharable system routines at runtime. This method enabled us to steal control of all runs of users who called the system routines. At the user's expense, we were able to covertly copy his files. Had we wanted to, we could have destroyed or selectively rewritten them.

COMMON FAILINGS OF OPERATING SYSTEM DESIGN

Operating systems are huge and complex sets of interacting programs. The current level of Exec VIII comprises about 500,000 lines of assembler code, and was written and modified by hundreds of programmers. We claim that no individual can understand such large and haphazardly constructed systems, and that such systems are bound to have holes. Emerging design techniques, such as "stepwise refinement," "hierarchical design," and "Parnas modularity" are sorely needed methods of keeping large programs comprehensible. Until such design techniques are routinely used for OS developments, large OS's will continue to be highly insecure.

Another characteristic impediment to the design of secure OS's is that many of the designers were trained on first and second generation systems, and their experience has resulted in an underestimation of the data security problem in a multiprogramming environment. . . .

WEAKNESSES OF EXEC VIII

[A] previous section described some of the design practices that result in programs that do not perform as specified. However, even if an MLS is completely bug-free, in the sense that its response to user requests is completely specified by its design, this does not imply that the MLS will not permit dissemination of data to unauthorized users. Our penetration of Exec VIII is not based on bugs in the implementation, though they certainly exist. Instead, we exploit several aspects of the Exec VIII design philosophy which, when taken together, make penetration possible. . . .

Under Exec VIII, there are a number of ways to construct environments for system routines which cause errors; the easiest is to place the bank of core that the routine uses as a data area lower or higher than the system routine "expects" it to be, causing a guard mode (memory reference out-of-bounds) error.

Unprotected Reentrant Processors. The problems of error recovery and environment checking converge to disastrous results in the case of sharable systems routines which are not part of the operating system (e.g., compilers, editors, and data base management systems). By and large, operating systems protect themselves from bad environments and cause error returns which do not give the user's calling task greater access than before the call, but such care has not been taken, under Exec VIII at least, to protect sharable nonexecutive routines. Such routines are called Reentrant Processors (REP's) on the 1108 because they are supposedly time-invariant (unmodifiable) program instructions and constants. A user requests the execution of a REP by means of an executive request, having previously prepared a core data area with the proper value. If an error occurs inside the REP, and the REP has not yet put in a request to handle its own errors, control will be returned to whichever task has requested to perform error handling. However, the task receiving control now has access to the REP, whereas before the link to the REP, it could not reference it.

Once the user has access to the REP, the 1108 cannot prevent a user from altering the core memory allocated to the REP. The reason for this is a hardware design oversight. 1108 hardware provides for write protection of both the instruction *and* data banks, or for neither. Since REP's, which are instruction banks, must be able to alter their associated data banks, the REP's themselves must run unprotected. This failure of memory protection in the case of REP's has been documented by Univac [5].

DETAILS OF THE SUBVERSION

These design errors in Exec VIII provide the basis for our method of illegal penetration. The program written to take advantage of the opportunities to subvert REP's offered by Exec VIII is composed of two tasks: a BREAKER, which gains access to the victim REP, and a

STEALER, which itself is a REP. Since we are interested in surreptitious entry, the highest priorities were to provide seemingly normal execution of the REP we were breaking and to structure the program so that *no* entries were written in the system log as a result of its execution. The function of the BREAKER is to prepare an out-of-bounds data bank for the victim REP and link to it, having previously requested to handle any resulting errors. The REP causes a guard mode error in trying to reference its data bank, and control returns to the BREAKER, but with access to the REP. The BREAKER changes the entry point of instruction of the REP to a jump to the end of the REP, where, as a result of the Exec VIII core allocation policy, there usually remain a number of unused words at the end of the last core block allocated to the REP.

The BREAKER then determines whether there are enough free words to enter a calling sequence to the STEALER and code to eradicate the visible effects of the call. If there is enough core, the BREAKER makes these changes; if not, it takes an error exit.

Sooner or later, the REP will lose its core allocation, and since they are supposedly unalterable, REP's are not swapped out, but only in. So the BREAKER must re-awaken periodically to see if the REP is still in core. If it is not, the BREAKER asks for it to be brought in again, and when it arrives, breaks it again. This cycle goes on until the machine goes down or the run is removed or a user links to the altered REP. The amount of processor time required to maintain the BREAKER is negligible; a run which kept the Univac assembler broken for about eight hours used thirteen seconds of processor time.

When a user links to the broken REP, control passes

through the calling sequence that the BREAKER added to the REP to our STEALER. It is evident that the STEALER must be a REP since many users may simultaneously link to the broken REP and end up in the STEALER. Also, the only easy way to make a routine accessible run boundaries is to make it a REP.

What the STEALER does when control from a user of the victim REP passes to it is immaterial; the penetration has already occurred. The STEALER has complete control of the user run and could:

1. Steal all assigned user files.
2. Destroy all assigned user files.
3. Selectively rewrite user files.
4. Terminate the user run.
5. Control any device assigned to the user.
6. Use all the machine time allocated to the user.

Since we are interested in covert entry, our STEALER merely steals assigned user files, writing them to one of our files. The STEALER then exists and control is returned to the victim REP with the user none the wiser....

When we began "production" runs, we were immediately faced with an information-pollution problem. We couldn't possibly manually look through all the files that we stole, so we developed a set of service routines to bring the stolen information into tractable form. We found that the file space required to store the stolen data was as large as one tenth of the total mass storage available on the 1108 system, and were forced again and again to restrict the class of users from whom the program would steal. At the end of the effort we only accepted data from classified users running in batch mode....

Bibliography

Allen, Brandt. "Embezzler's Guide to the Computer." *Harvard Business Review,* Vol. 53 (July–August 1975).

Baird, Lindsay L., Jr. "How to Identify Computer Vulnerability." *Magazine of Bank Administration,* Vol. 50 (October 1974).

Becker, Robert S. *The Data Processing Security Game.* New York: Pergamon Press, 1977.

Bequai, August. *Computer Crime.* Lexington, Mass.: Lexington Books, 1977.

Bequai, August. *White Collar Crime.* Lexington, Mass.: Lexington Books, 1978.

Bequai, August. "The Cashless Society: An Analysis of the Threat of Crime and Invasion of Privacy." Utah University Journal of Contemporary Law, Vol. 3 (1976).

Branstad, Dennis K. "Data Protection Through Cryptography." *Dimensions* (National Bureau of Standards), Vol. 50 (September 1975).

Browne, Peter S. "Computer Security—A Survey." *Proceedings of the National Computer Conference.* Association for Computing Machinery (June 1976).

Feistel, Horst. "Cryptography and Computer Privacy." *Scientific American,* May 1973.

Greene, Richard. *Business Intelligence and Espionage.* Homewood, Ill.: Dow Jones–Irwin, 1966.

Hoffman, Lance. *Modern Methods for Computer Security and Privacy.* Englewood Cliffs, N.J.: Prentice-Hall, 1977.

Kahn, David. *The Codebreakers.* New York: Macmillan, 1967.

Mair, William, and others. *Computer Control and Audit.* Altamonte Springs, Fla.: Institute of Internal Auditors.

Martin, James. *Security, Accuracy and Privacy in Computer Systems.* Englewood Cliffs, N.J.: Prentice-Hall, 1973.

McKnight, Gerald. *Computer Crime.* New York: Walker & Co., 1973.

National Science Foundation. *The Consequences of Electronic Funds Transfer.* Washington, D.C.: Government Printing Office, 1975.

Parker, Donn B. *Crime by Computer.* New York: Scribner, 1976.

Parker, Donn B. "A Look at Computer Fraud and Embezzlement in Banking." *Bank Administration,* May 1976.

Seidler, Lee, and others. *The Equity Funding Papers: The Anatomy of a Fraud.* New York: Wiley, 1977.

U.S. Senate, Committee on Government Operations. *Staff Study of Computer Security in Federal Programs.* Washington, D.C.: Government Printing Office, 1976.